Beowulf

with Related Readings

Glencoe
McGraw-Hill

New York, New York   Columbus, Ohio   Woodland Hills, California   Peoria, Illinois

Acknowledgments

Grateful acknowledgment is given authors, publishers, photographers, museums, and agents for permission to reprint the following copyrighted material. Every effort has been made to determine copyright owners. In case of any omissions, the Publisher will be pleased to make suitable acknowledgments in future editions.

Beowulf, translated by Burton Raffel. Translation copyright © Burton Raffel, 1963. Translation copyright renewed © Burton Raffel, 1991. Published by arrangement with NAL Signet, a division of Penguin Putnam Inc.

Excerpt from Seamus Heaney interview with Elizabeth Farnsworth. NewsHour with Jim Lehrer, March 28, 2000. Copyright © 2000 MacNeil/Lehrer Productions. Reprinted by permission.

From *Grendel* by John Gardner. Copyright © 1971 by John Gardner. Reprinted by permission of Alfred A. Knopf, a Division of Random House, Inc.

"Anchor," "Fish in River" and "Shield" from *An Anthology of Old English Poetry*, translated into alliterative verse by Charles W. Kennedy. Copyright © 1960 Oxford University Press. Reprinted by permission.

"The Slaying" from *Catastrophe and Other Stories* by Dino Buzzati, translated by Judith Landry and Cynthia Jolly. Copyright © 1949, 1954, 1958 by Arnoldo Mondadori Editore, Milano. Translations copyright © 1965, Calders and Boyars. Reprinted by permission of Riverrun Press, New York.

Excerpt from *Her Kind* by Jane Cahill. Copyright © 1995 by Jane Cahill. Reprinted by permission of Broadview Press.

"The Woman with the Big Thumbnail" from *Tales from the Basotho*, by Minnie Postma, translated from Afrikaans by Susie McDermid. Copyright © 1964 by Afrikaanse Pers-Boekhandel. Copyright © 1974 by the American Folklore Society. Reprinted by permission.

Cover Art: Vendel Warrior's Helmet, 7th century Viking, Art Resource.

Glencoe/McGraw-Hill

A Division of The **McGraw·Hill** Companies

Send all inquiries to:
Glencoe/McGraw-Hill
8787 Orion Place
Columbus, OH 43240

ISBN 0-07-823545-6
Printed in the United States of America
4 5 6 7 8 9 10   026   10 09 08

Contents

Beowulf

Translated by
Burton Raffel

Beowulf

Prologue

    Hear me! We've heard of Danish heroes,
Ancient kings and the glory they cut
For themselves, swinging mighty swords!
    How Shild made slaves of soldiers from every
5   Land, crowds of captives he'd beaten
Into terror; he'd traveled to Denmark alone,
An abandoned child, but changed his own fate,
Lived to be rich and much honored. He ruled
Lands on all sides: wherever the sea
10   Would take them his soldiers sailed, returned
With tribute and obedience. There was a brave
King! And he gave them more than his glory,
Conceived a son for the Danes, a new leader
Allowed them by the grace of God. They had lived,
15   Before his coming, kingless and miserable;
Now the Lord of all life, Ruler
Of glory, blessed them with a prince, Beo,
Whose power and fame soon spread through the
       world.
Shild's strong son was the glory of Denmark;
20   His father's warriors were wound round his heart
With golden rings bound to their prince
By his father's treasure. So young men build
The future, wisely open-handed in peace,
Protected in war; so warriors earn
25   Their fame, and wealth is shaped with a sword.
    When his time was come the old king died,
Still strong but called to the Lord's hands.
His comrades carried him down to the shore,
Bore him as their leader had asked, their lord
And companion while words could move on his
30   tongue.
Shild's reign had been long; he'd ruled them well.

There in the harbor was a ring-prowed fighting
Ship, its timbers icy, waiting,
And there they brought the belovèd body
35 Of their ring-giving lord, and laid him near
The mast. Next to that noble corpse
They heaped up treasures, jeweled helmets,
Hooked swords and coats of mail, armor
Carried from the ends of the earth: no ship
40 Had ever sailed so brightly fitted,
No king sent forth more deeply mourned.
Forced to set him adrift, floating
As far as the tide might run, they refused
To give him less from their hoards of gold
45 Than those who'd shipped him away, an orphan
And a beggar, to cross the waves alone.
High up over his head they flew
His shining banner, then sadly let
The water pull at the ship, watched it
50 Slowly sliding to where neither rulers
Nor heroes nor anyone can say whose hands
Opened to take that motionless cargo.

1

Then Beo was king in that Danish castle,
Shild's son ruling as long as his father
55 And as loved, a famous lord of men.
And he in turn gave his people a son,
The great Healfdane, a fierce fighter
Who led the Danes to the end of his long
Life and left them four children,
60 Three princes to guide them in battle, Hergar
And Hrothgar and Halga the Good, and one
daughter,
Yrs, who was given to Onela, king
Of the Swedes, and became his wife and their queen.
Then Hrothgar, taking the throne, led
65 The Danes to such glory that comrades and kinsmen
Swore by his sword, and young men swelled
His armies, and he thought of greatness and resolved
To build a hall that would hold his mighty
Band and reach higher toward Heaven than anything
70 That had ever been known to the sons of men.
And in that hall he'd divide the spoils
Of their victories, to old and young what they'd
earned
In battle, but leaving the common pastures
Untouched, and taking no lives. The work
75 Was ordered, the timbers tied and shaped
By the hosts that Hrothgar ruled. It was quickly
Ready, that most beautiful of dwellings, built
As he'd wanted, and then he whose word was obeyed
All over the earth named it Herot.
80 His boast come true he commanded a banquet,
Opened out his treasure-full hands.
That towering place, gabled and huge,
Stood waiting for time to pass, for war
To begin, for flames to leap as high
As the feud that would light them, and for Herot to
85 burn.
A powerful monster, living down
In the darkness, growled in pain, impatient
As day after day the music rang
Loud in that hall, the harp's rejoicing

90   Call and the poet's clear songs, sung
Of the ancient beginnings of us all, recalling
The Almighty making the earth, shaping
These beautiful plains marked off by oceans,
Then proudly setting the sun and moon
95   To glow across the land and light it;
The corners of the earth were made lovely with trees
And leaves, made quick with life, with each
Of the nations who now move on its face. And then
As now warriors sang of their pleasure:
100   So Hrothgar's men lived happy in his hall
Till the monster stirred, that demon, that fiend,
Grendel, who haunted the moors, the wild
Marshes, and made his home in a hell
Not hell but earth. He was spawned in that slime,
105   Conceived by a pair of those monsters born
Of Cain, murderous creatures banished
By God, punished forever for the crime
Of Abel's death. The Almighty drove
Those demons out, and their exile was bitter,
110   Shut away from men; they split
Into a thousand forms of evil—spirits
And fiends, goblins, monsters, giants,
A brood forever opposing the Lord's
Will, and again and again defeated.

2

115   Then, when darkness had dropped, Grendel
Went up to Herot, wondering what the warriors
Would do in that hall when their drinking was done.
He found them sprawled in sleep, suspecting
Nothing, their dreams undisturbed. The monster's
120   Thoughts were as quick as his greed or his claws:
He slipped through the door and there in the silence
Snatched up thirty men, smashed them

Unknowing in their beds and ran out with their
    bodies,
The blood dripping behind him, back
125 To his lair, delighted with his night's slaughter.
    At daybreak, with the sun's first light, they saw
How well he had worked, and in that gray morning
Broke their long feast with tears and laments
For the dead. Hrothgar, their lord, sat joyless
130 In Herot, a mighty prince mourning
The fate of his lost friends and companions,
Knowing by its tracks that some demon had torn
His followers apart. He wept, fearing
The beginning might not be the end. And that night
135 Grendel came again, so set
On murder that no crime could ever be enough,
No savage assault quench his lust
For evil. Then each warrior tried
To escape him, searched for rest in different
140 Beds, as far from Herot as they could find,
Seeing how Grendel hunted when they slept.
Distance was safety; the only survivors
Were those who fled him. Hate had triumphed.
    So Grendel ruled, fought with the righteous,
145 One against many, and won; so Herot
Stood empty, and stayed deserted for years,
Twelve winters of grief for Hrothgar, king
Of the Danes, sorrow heaped at his door
By hell-forged hands. His misery leaped
150 The seas, was told and sung in all
Men's ears: how Grendel's hatred began,
How the monster relished his savage war
On the Danes, keeping the bloody feud
Alive, seeking no peace, offering
155 No truce, accepting no settlement, no price
In gold or land, and paying the living
For one crime only with another. No one
Waited for reparation from his plundering claws:
That shadow of death hunted in the darkness,
160 Stalked Hrothgar's warriors, old
And young, lying in waiting, hidden
In mist, invisibly following them from the edge
Of the marsh, always there, unseen.

So mankind's enemy continued his crimes,
165 Killing as often as he could, coming
Alone, bloodthirsty and horrible. Though he lived
In Herot, when the night hid him, he never
Dared to touch king Hrothgar's glorious
Throne, protected by God—God,
170 Whose love Grendel could not know. But Hrothgar's
Heart was bent. The best and most noble
Of his council debated remedies, sat
In secret sessions, talking of terror
And wondering what the bravest of warriors could do.
175 And sometimes they sacrificed to the old stone gods,
Made heathen vows, hoping for Hell's
Support, the Devil's guidance in driving
Their affliction off. That was their way,
And the heathen's only hope, Hell
180 Always in their hearts, knowing neither God
Nor His passing as He walks through our world, the
     Lord
Of Heaven and earth; their ears could not hear
His praise nor know His glory. Let them
Beware, those who are thrust into danger,
185 Clutched at by trouble, yet can carry no solace
In their hearts, cannot hope to be better! Hail
To those who will rise to God, drop off
Their dead bodies and seek our Father's peace!

3

So the living sorrow of Healfdane's son
190 Simmered, bitter and fresh, and no wisdom
Or strength could break it: that agony hung
On King and people alike, harsh
And unending, violent and cruel, and evil.
     In his far-off home Beowulf, Higlac's
195 Follower and the strongest of the Geats—greater
And stronger than anyone anywhere in this world—

Heard how Grendel filled nights with horror
And quickly commanded a boat fitted out,
Proclaiming that he'd go to that famous king,
200 Would sail across the sea to Hrothgar,
Now when help was needed. None
Of the wise ones regretted his going, much
As he was loved by the Geats: the omens were good,
And they urged the adventure on. So Beowulf
205 Chose the mightiest men he could find,
The bravest and best of the Geats, fourteen
In all, and led them down to their boat;
He knew the sea, would point the prow
Straight to that distant Danish shore.
210   Then they sailed, set their ship
Out on the waves, under the cliffs.
Ready for what came they wound through the
        currents,
The seas beating at the sand, and were borne
In the lap of their shining ship, lined
215 With gleaming armor, going safely
In that oak-hard boat to where their hearts took
        them.
The wind hurried them over the waves,
The ship foamed through the sea like a bird
Until, in the time they had known it would take,
220 Standing in the round-curled prow they could see
Sparkling hills, high and green,
Jutting up over the shore, and rejoicing
In those rock-steep cliffs they quietly ended
Their voyage. Jumping to the ground, the Geats
225 Pushed their boat to the sand and tied it
In place, mail shirts and armor rattling
As they swiftly moored their ship. And then
They gave thanks to God for their easy crossing.
        High on a wall a Danish watcher
230 Patrolling along the cliffs saw
The travelers crossing to the shore, their shields
Raised and shining; he came riding down,
Hrothgar's lieutenant, spurring his horse,
Needing to know why they'd landed, these men
235 In armor. Shaking his heavy spear
In their faces he spoke:

"Whose soldiers are you,
You who've been carried in your deep-keeled ship
Across the sea-road to this country of mine?
240 Listen! I've stood on these cliffs longer
Than you know, keeping our coast free
Of pirates, raiders sneaking ashore
From their ships, seeking our lives and our gold.
None have ever come more openly—
245 And yet you've offered no password, no sign
From my prince, no permission from my people for
    your landing
Here. Nor have I ever seen,
Out of all the men on earth, one greater
Than has come with you; no commoner carries
250 Such weapons, unless his appearance, and his beauty,
Are both lies. You! Tell me your name,
And your father's; no spies go further onto Danish
Soil than you've come already. Strangers,
From wherever it was you sailed, tell it,
255 And tell it quickly, the quicker the better,
I say, for us all. Speak, say
Exactly who you are, and from where, and why."

4

Their leader answered him, Beowulf unlocking
Words from deep in his breast:
260   "We are Geats,
Men who follow Higlac. My father
Was a famous soldier, known far and wide
As a leader of men. His name was Edgetho.
His life lasted many winters;
265 Wise men all over the earth surely
Remember him still. And we have come seeking
Your prince, Healfdane's son, protector
Of this people, only in friendship: instruct us,
Watchman, help us with your words! Our errand

270 Is a great one, our business with the glorious king
Of the Danes no secret; there's nothing dark
Or hidden in our coming. You know (if we've heard
The truth, and been told honestly) that your country
Is cursed with some strange, vicious creature
275 That hunts only at night and that no one
Has seen. It's said, watchman, that he has slaughtered
Your people, brought terror to the darkness. Perhaps
Hrothgar can hunt, here in my heart,
For some way to drive this devil out—
280 If anything will ever end the evils
Afflicting your wise and famous lord.
Here he can cool his burning sorrow.
Or else he may see his suffering go on
Forever, for as long as Herot towers
285 High on your hills."
        The mounted officer
Answered him bluntly, the brave watchman:
  "A soldier should know the difference between
   words
And deeds, and keep that knowledge clear
290 In his brain. I believe your words, I trust in
Your friendship. Go forward, weapons and armor
And all, on into Denmark. I'll guide you
Myself—and my men will guard your ship,
Keep it safe here on our shores,
295 Your fresh-tarred boat, watch it well,
Until that curving prow carries
Across the sea to Geatland a chosen
Warrior who bravely does battle with the creature
Haunting our people, who survives that horror
300 Unhurt, and goes home bearing our love."
  Then they moved on. Their boat lay moored,
Tied tight to its anchor. Glittering at the top
Of their golden helmets wild boar heads gleamed,
Shining decorations, swinging as they marched,
305 Erect like guards, like sentinels, as though ready
To fight. They marched, Beowulf and his men
And their guide, until they could see the gables
Of Herot, covered with hammered gold
And glowing in the sun—that most famous of all
   dwellings,

310 Towering majestic, its glittering roofs
Visible far across the land.
Their guide reined in his horse, pointing
To that hall, built by Hrothgar for the best
And bravest of his men; the path was plain,
315 They could see their way. And then he spoke:
"Now I must leave you: may the Lord our God
Protect your coming and going! The sea
Is my job, keeping these coasts free
Of invaders, bands of pirates: I must go back."

5

320 The path he'd shown them was paved, cobbled
Like a Roman road. They arrived with their mail shirts
Glittering, silver-shining links
Clanking an iron song as they came.
Sea-weary still, they set their broad,
325 Battle-hardened shields in rows
Along the wall, then stretched themselves
On Herot's benches. Their armor rang;
Their ash-wood spears stood in a line,
Gray-tipped and straight: the Geats' war-gear
330 Were honored weapons.
                         A Danish warrior
Asked who they were, their names and their fathers':
    "Where have you carried these gold-carved shields
        from,
These silvery shirts and helmets, and those spears
335 Set out in long lines? I am Hrothgar's
Herald and captain. Strangers have come here
Before, but never so freely, so bold.
And you come too proudly to be exiles: not poverty
But your hearts' high courage has brought you to
        Hrothgar."
340 He was answered by a famous soldier, the Geats'
Proud prince:

          "We follow Higlac, break bread
        At his side. I am Beowulf. My errand
        Is for Healfdane's great son to hear, your glorious
345   Lord; if he chooses to receive us we will greet him,
        Salute the chief of the Danes and speak out
        Our message."
                        Wulfgar replied—a prince
        Born to the Swedes, famous for both strength
350   And wisdom:
                        "Our warmhearted lord will be told
        Of your coming; I shall tell our king, our giver
        Of bright rings, and hurry back with his word,
        And speak it here, however he answers
355   Your request."
                        He went quickly to where Hrothgar
            sat,
        Gray and old, in the middle of his men,
        And knowing the custom of that court walked straight
        To the king's great chair, stood waiting to be heard,
360   Then spoke:
                        "There are Geats who have come sailing
            the open
        Ocean to our land, come far over
        The high waves, led by a warrior
        Called Beowulf. They wait on your word, bring
            messages
365   For your ears alone. My lord, grant them
        A gracious answer, see them and hear
        What they've come for! Their weapons and armor are
            nobly
        Worked—these men are no beggars. And Beowulf
        Their prince, who showed them the way to our shores,
370   Is a mighty warrior, powerful and wise."

6

The Danes' high prince and protector answered:
"I knew Beowulf as a boy. His father
Was Edgetho, who was given Hrethel's one daughter
—Hrethel, Higlac's father. Now Edgetho's

375 Brave son is here, come visiting a friendly
King. And I've heard that when seamen came,
Bringing their gifts and presents to the Geats,
They wrestled and ran together, and Higlac's
Young prince showed them a mighty battle-grip,

380 Hands that moved with thirty men's strength,
And courage to match. Our Holy Father
Has sent him as a sign of His grace, a mark
Of His favor, to help us defeat Grendel
And end that terror. I shall greet him with treasures,

385 Gifts to reward his courage in coming to us.
Quickly, order them all to come to me
Together, Beowulf and his band of Geats.
And tell them, too, how welcome we will make
          them!"
          Then Wulfgar went to the door and addressed

390 The waiting seafarers with soldier's words:
          "My lord, the great king of the Danes, commands
          me
To tell you that he knows of your noble birth
And that having come to him from over the open
Sea you have come bravely and are welcome.

395 Now go to him as you are, in your armor and helmets,
But leave your battle-shields here, and your spears,
Let them lie waiting for the promises your words
May make."
          Beowulf arose, with his men

400 Around him, ordering a few to remain
With their weapons, leading the others quickly
Along under Herot's steep roof into Hrothgar's
Presence. Standing on that prince's own hearth,
Helmeted, the silvery metal of his mail shirt

405 Gleaming with a smith's high art, he greeted
The Danes' great lord:
                    "Hail, Hrothgar!
Higlac is my cousin and my king; the days

Of my youth have been filled with glory. Now Grendel's

410 Name has echoed in our land: sailors
Have brought us stories of Herot, the best
Of all mead-halls, deserted and useless when the moon
Hangs in skies the sun had lit,
Light and life fleeing together.

415 My people have said, the wisest, most knowing
And best of them, that my duty was to go to the Danes'
Great king. They have seen my strength for themselves,
Have watched me rise from the darkness of war,
Dripping with my enemies' blood. I drove

420 Five great giants into chains, chased
All of that race from the earth. I swam
In the blackness of night, hunting monsters
Out of the ocean, and killing them one
By one; death was my errand and the fate

425 They had earned. Now Grendel and I are called
Together, and I've come. Grant me, then,
Lord and protector of this noble place,
A single request! I have come so far,
Oh shelterer of warriors and your people's loved friend,

430 That this one favor you should not refuse me—
That I, alone and with the help of my men,
May purge all evil from this hall. I have heard,
Too, that the monster's scorn of men
Is so great that he needs no weapons and fears none.

435 Nor will I. My lord Higlac
Might think less of me if I let my sword
Go where my feet were afraid to, if I hid
Behind some broad linden shield: my hands
Alone shall fight for me, struggle for life

440 Against the monster. God must decide
Who will be given to death's cold grip.
Grendel's plan, I think, will be
What it has been before, to invade this hall
And gorge his belly with our bodies. If he can,

445 If he can. And I think, if my time will have come,

There'll be nothing to mourn over, no corpse to
    prepare
For its grave: Grendel will carry our bloody
Flesh to the moors, crunch on our bones
And smear torn scraps of our skin on the walls
450   Of his den. No, I expect no Danes
Will fret about sewing our shrouds, if he wins.
And if death does take me, send the hammered
Mail of my armor to Higlac, return
The inheritance I had from Hrethel, and he
455   From Wayland. Fate will unwind as it must!"

7

Hrothgar replied, protector of the Danes:
    "Beowulf, you've come to us in friendship, and
        because
Of the reception your father found at our court.
Edgetho had begun a bitter feud,
460   Killing Hathlaf, a Wulfing warrior:
Your father's countrymen were afraid of war,
If he returned to his home, and they turned him away.
Then he traveled across the curving waves
To the land of the Danes. I was new to the throne,
465   Then, a young man ruling this wide
Kingdom and its golden city: Hergar,
My older brother, a far better man
Than I, had died and dying made me,
Second among Healfdane's sons, first
470   In this nation. I bought the end of Edgetho's
Quarrel, sent ancient treasures through the ocean's
Furrows to the Wulfings; your father swore
He'd keep that peace. My tongue grows heavy,
And my heart, when I try to tell you what Grendel
475   Has brought us, the damage he's done, here
In this hall. You see for yourself how much smaller

Our ranks have become, and can guess what we've
    lost
To his terror. Surely the Lord Almighty
Could stop his madness, smother his lust!
480   How many times have my men, glowing
With courage drawn from too many cups
Of ale, sworn to stay after dark
And stem that horror with a sweep of their swords.
And then, in the morning, this mead-hall glittering
485   With new light would be drenched with blood, the
    benches
Stained red, the floors, all wet from that fiend's
Savage assault—and my soldiers would be fewer
Still, death taking more and more.
But to table, Beowulf, a banquet in your honor:
490   Let us toast your victories, and talk of the future."
       Then Hrothgar's men gave places to the Geats,
Yielded benches to the brave visitors
And led them to the feast. The keeper of the mead
Came carrying out the carved flasks,
495   And poured that bright sweetness. A poet
Sang, from time to time, in a clear
Pure voice. Danes and visiting Geats
Celebrated as one, drank and rejoiced.

8

      Unferth spoke, Ecglaf's son,
500   Who sat at Hrothgar's feet, spoke harshly
And sharp (vexed by Beowulf's adventure,
By their visitor's courage, and angry that anyone
In Denmark or anywhere on earth had ever
Acquired glory and fame greater
505   Than his own):
                "You're Beowulf, are you—the same
Boastful fool who fought a swimming
Match with Brecca, both of you daring

And young and proud, exploring the deepest
510 Seas, risking your lives for no reason
But the danger? All older and wiser heads warned you
Not to, but no one could check such pride.
With Brecca at your side you swam along
The sea-paths, your swift-moving hands pulling you
515 Over the ocean's face. Then winter
Churned through the water, the waves ran you
As they willed, and you struggled seven long nights
To survive. And at the end victory was his,
Not yours. The sea carried him close
520 To his home, to southern Norway, near
The land of the Brondings, where he ruled and was
         loved,
Where his treasure was piled and his strength
         protected
His towns and his people. He'd promised to outswim
         you:
Bonstan's son made that boast ring true.
525 You've been lucky in your battles, Beowulf, but I think
Your luck may change if you challenge Grendel,
Staying a whole night through in this hall,
Waiting where that fiercest of demons can find you."
     Beowulf answered, Edgetho's great son:
530   "Ah! Unferth, my friend, your face
Is hot with ale, and your tongue has tried
To tell us about Brecca's doings. But the truth
Is simple: no man swims in the sea
As I can, no strength is a match for mine.
535 As boys, Brecca and I had boasted—
We were both too young to know better—that we'd
         risk
Our lives far out at sea, and so
We did. Each of us carried a naked
Sword, prepared for whales or the swift
540 Sharp teeth and beaks of needlefish.
He could never leave me behind, swim faster
Across the waves than I could, and I
Had chosen to remain close to his side.
I remained near him for five long nights,
545 Until a flood swept us apart;
The frozen sea surged around me,

It grew dark, the wind turned bitter, blowing
From the north, and the waves were savage. Creatures
Who sleep deep in the sea were stirred
550 Into life—and the iron hammered links
Of my mail shirt, these shining bits of metal
Woven across my breast, saved me
From death. A monster seized me, drew me
Swiftly toward the bottom, swimming with its claws
555 Tight in my flesh. But fate let me
Find its heart with my sword, hack myself
Free; I fought that beast's last battle,
Left it floating lifeless in the sea.

9

"Other monsters crowded around me,
560 Continually attacking. I treated them politely,
Offering the edge of my razor-sharp sword.
But the feast, I think, did not please them, filled
Their evil bellies with no banquet-rich food,
Thrashing there at the bottom of the sea;
565 By morning they'd decided to sleep on the shore,
Lying on their backs, their blood spilled out
On the sand. Afterwards, sailors could cross
That sea-road and feel no fear; nothing
Would stop their passing. Then God's bright beacon
570 Appeared in the east, the water lay still,
And at last I could see the land, wind-swept
Cliff-walls at the edge of the coast. Fate saves
The living when they drive away death by
        themselves!
Lucky or not, nine was the number
575 Of sea-huge monsters I killed. What man,
Anywhere under Heaven's high arch, has fought
In such darkness, endured more misery or been harder
Pressed? Yet I survived the sea, smashed
The monsters' hot jaws, swam home from my journey.

580 The swift-flowing waters swept me along
And I landed on Finnish soil. I've heard
No tales of you, Unferth, telling
Of such clashing terror, such contests in the night!
Brecca's battles were never so bold;
585 Neither he nor you can match me—and I mean
No boast, have announced no more than I know
To be true. And there's more: you murdered your
                brothers,
Your own close kin. Words and bright wit
Won't help your soul; you'll suffer hell's fires,
590 Unferth, forever tormented. Ecglaf's
Proud son, if your hands were as hard, your heart
As fierce as you think it, no fool would dare
To raid your hall, ruin Herot
And oppress its prince, as Grendel has done.
595 But he's learned that terror is his alone,
Discovered he can come for your people with no fear
Of reprisal; he's found no fighting, here,
But only food, only delight.
He murders as he likes, with no mercy, gorges
600 And feasts on your flesh, and expects no trouble,
No quarrel from the quiet Danes. Now
The Geats will show him courage, soon
He can test his strength in battle. And when the sun
Comes up again, opening another
605 Bright day from the south, anyone in Denmark
May enter this hall: that evil will be gone!"
    Hrothgar, gray-haired and brave, sat happily
Listening, the famous ring-giver sure,
At last, that Grendel could be killed; he believed
610 In Beowulf's bold strength and the firmness of his
                spirit.
    There was the sound of laughter, and the cheerful
                clanking
Of cups, and pleasant words. Then Welthow,
Hrothgar's gold-ringed queen, greeted
The warriors; a noble woman who knew
615 What was right, she raised a flowing cup
To Hrothgar first, holding it high
For the lord of the Danes to drink, wishing him
Joy in that feast. The famous king

Drank with pleasure and blessed their banquet.

620 Then Welthow went from warrior to warrior,
Pouring a portion from the jeweled cup
For each, till the bracelet-wearing queen
Had carried the mead-cup among them and it was
      Beowulf's
Turn to be served. She saluted the Geats'

625 Great prince, thanked God for answering her prayers,
For allowing her hands the happy duty
Of offering mead to a hero who would help
Her afflicted people. He drank what she poured,
Edgetho's brave son, then assured the Danish

630 Queen that his heart was firm and his hands
Ready:
      "When we crossed the sea, my comrades
And I, I already knew that all
My purpose was this: to win the good will

635 Of your people or die in battle, pressed
In Grendel's fierce grip. Let me live in greatness
And courage, or here in this hall welcome
My death!"
      Welthow was pleased with his words,

640 His bright-tongued boasts; she carried them back
To her lord, walked nobly across to his side.
    The feast went on, laughter and music
And the brave words of warriors celebrating
Their delight. Then Hrothgar rose, Healfdane's

645 Son, heavy with sleep; as soon
As the sun had gone, he knew that Grendel
Would come to Herot, would visit that hall
When night had covered the earth with its net
And the shapes of darkness moved black and silent

650 Through the world. Hrothgar's warriors rose with him.
    He went to Beowulf, embraced the Geats'
Brave prince, wished him well, and hoped
That Herot would be his to command. And then
He declared:

655   "No one strange to this land
Has ever been granted what I've given you,
No one in all the years of my rule.
Make this best of all mead-halls yours, and then
Keep it free of evil, fight

660 With glory in your heart! Purge Herot
And your ship will sail home with its treasure-holds
full."

10

Then Hrothgar left that hall, the Danes'
Great protector, followed by his court; the queen
Had preceded him and he went to lie at her side,
665 Seek sleep near his wife. It was said that God
Himself had set a sentinel in Herot,
Brought Beowulf as a guard against Grendel and a
shield
Behind whom the king could safely rest.
And Beowulf was ready, firm with our Lord's
670 High favor and his own bold courage and strength.
He stripped off his mail shirt, his helmet, his sword
Hammered from the hardest iron, and handed
All his weapons and armor to a servant,
Ordered his war-gear guarded till morning.
675 And then, standing beside his bed,
He exclaimed:
"Grendel is no braver, no stronger
Than I am! I could kill him with my sword; I shall
not,
Easy as it would be. This fiend is a bold
680 And famous fighter, but his claws and teeth
Scratching at my shield, his clumsy fists
Beating at my sword blade, would be helpless. I
will meet him
With my hands empty—unless his heart
Fails him, seeing a soldier waiting
685 Weaponless, unafraid. Let God in His wisdom
Extend His hand where He wills, reward
Whom He chooses!"
Then the Geats' great chief
dropped

His head to his pillow, and around him, as ready
690 As they could be, lay the soldiers who had crossed the
sea
At his side, each of them sure that he was lost
To the home he loved, to the high-walled towns
And the friends he had left behind where both he
And they had been raised. Each thought of the
Danes
695 Murdered by Grendel in a hall where Geats
And not Danes now slept. But God's dread loom
Was woven with defeat for the monster, good fortune
For the Geats; help against Grendel was with them,
And through the might of a single man
700 They would win. Who doubts that God in His wisdom
And strength holds the earth forever
In His hands? Out in the darkness the monster
Began to walk. The warriors slept
In that gabled hall where they hoped that He
705 Would keep them safe from evil, guard them
From death till the end of their days was determined
And the thread should be broken. But Beowulf lay
wakeful,
Watching, waiting, eager to meet
His enemy, and angry at the thought of his coming.

11

710 Out from the marsh, from the foot of misty
Hills and bogs, bearing God's hatred,
Grendel came, hoping to kill
Anyone he could trap on this trip to high Herot.
He moved quickly through the cloudy night,
715 Up from his swampland, sliding silently
Toward that gold-shining hall. He had visited
Hrothgar's
Home before, knew the way—
But never, before nor after that night,

Found Herot defended so firmly, his reception
720 So harsh. He journeyed, forever joyless,
Straight to the door, then snapped it open,
Tore its iron fasteners with a touch
And rushed angrily over the threshold.
He strode quickly across the inlaid
725 Floor, snarling and fierce: his eyes
Gleamed in the darkness, burned with a gruesome
Light. Then he stopped, seeing the hall
Crowded with sleeping warriors, stuffed
With rows of young soldiers resting together.
730 And his heart laughed, he relished the sight,
Intended to tear the life from those bodies
By morning; the monster's mind was hot
With the thought of food and the feasting his belly
Would soon know. But fate, that night, intended
735 Grendel to gnaw the broken bones
Of his last human supper. Human
Eyes were watching his evil steps,
Waiting to see his swift hard claws.
Grendel snatched at the first Geat
740 He came to, ripped him apart, cut
His body to bits with powerful jaws,
Drank the blood from his veins and bolted
Him down, hands and feet; death
And Grendel's great teeth came together,
745 Snapping life shut. Then he stepped to another
Still body, clutched at Beowulf with his claws,
Grasped at a strong-hearted wakeful sleeper
—And was instantly seized himself, claws
Bent back as Beowulf leaned up on one arm.
750 That shepherd of evil, guardian of crime,
Knew at once that nowhere on earth
Had he met a man whose hands were harder;
His mind was flooded with fear—but nothing
Could take his talons and himself from that tight
755 Hard grip. Grendel's one thought was to run
From Beowulf, flee back to his marsh and hide
there:
This was a different Herot than the hall he had
emptied.
But Higlac's follower remembered his final

Boast and, standing erect, stopped
760 The monster's flight, fastened those claws
In his fists till they cracked, clutched Grendel
Closer. The infamous killer fought
For his freedom, wanting no flesh but retreat,
Desiring nothing but escape; his claws
765 Had been caught, he was trapped. That trip to
Herot
Was a miserable journey for the writhing monster!
The high hall rang, its roof boards swayed,
And Danes shook with terror. Down
The aisles the battle swept, angry
770 And wild, Herot trembled, wonderfully
Built to withstand the blows, the struggling
Great bodies beating at its beautiful walls;
Shaped and fastened with iron, inside
And out, artfully worked, the building
775 Stood firm. Its benches rattled, fell
To the floor, gold-covered boards grating
As Grendel and Beowulf battled across them.
Hrothgar's wise men had fashioned Herot
To stand forever; only fire,
780 They had planned, could shatter what such skill
had put
Together, swallow in hot flames such splendor
Of ivory and iron and wood. Suddenly
The sounds changed, the Danes started
In new terror, cowering in their beds as the terrible
785 Screams of the Almighty's enemy sang
In the darkness, the horrible shrieks of pain
And defeat, the tears torn out of Grendel's
Taut throat, hell's captive caught in the arms
Of him who of all the men on earth
790 Was the strongest.

12

That mighty protector of men
Meant to hold the monster till its life
Leaped out, knowing the fiend was no use
To anyone in Denmark. All of Beowulf's
795   Band had jumped from their beds, ancestral
Swords raised and ready, determined
To protect their prince if they could. Their courage
Was great but all wasted: they could hack at Grendel
From every side, trying to open
800   A path for his evil soul, but their points
Could not hurt him, the sharpest and hardest iron
Could not scratch at his skin, for that sin-stained
     demon
Had bewitched all men's weapons, laid spells
That blunted every mortal man's blade.
805   And yet his time had come, his days
Were over, his death near; down
To hell he would go, swept groaning and helpless
To the waiting hands of still worse fiends.
Now he discovered—once the afflictor
810   Of men, tormentor of their days—what it meant
To feud with Almighty God: Grendel
Saw that his strength was deserting him, his claws
Bound fast, Higlac's brave follower tearing at
His hands. The monster's hatred rose higher,
815   But his power had gone. He twisted in pain,
And the bleeding sinews deep in his shoulder
Snapped, muscle and bone split
And broke. The battle was over, Beowulf
Had been granted new glory: Grendel escaped,
820   But wounded as he was could flee to his den,
His miserable hole at the bottom of the marsh,
Only to die, to wait for the end
Of all his days. And after that bloody
Combat the Danes laughed with delight.
825   He who had come to them from across the sea,
Bold and strong-minded, had driven affliction
Off, purged Herot clean. He was happy,
Now, with that night's fierce work; the Danes

Had been served as he'd boasted he'd serve them; Beowulf,

830 A prince of the Geats, had killed Grendel,
Ended the grief, the sorrow, the suffering
Forced on Hrothgar's helpless people
By a bloodthirsty fiend. No Dane doubted
The victory, for the proof, hanging high
835 From the rafters where Beowulf had hung it, was the monster's
Arm, claw and shoulder and all.

13

And then, in the morning, crowds surrounded
Herot, warriors coming to that hall
From faraway lands, princes and leaders
840 Of men hurrying to behold the monster's
Great staggering tracks. They gaped with no sense
Of sorrow, felt no regret for his suffering,
Went tracing his bloody footprints, his beaten
And lonely flight, to the edge of the lake
845 Where he'd dragged his corpselike way, doomed
And already weary of his vanishing life.
The water was bloody, steaming and boiling
In horrible pounding waves, heat
Sucked from his magic veins; but the swirling
850 Surf had covered his death, hidden
Deep in murky darkness his miserable
End, as hell opened to receive him.
Then old and young rejoiced, turned back
From that happy pilgrimage, mounted their hard-hooved
855 Horses, high-spirited stallions, and rode them
Slowly toward Herot again, retelling
Beowulf's bravery as they jogged along.
And over and over they swore that nowhere
On earth or under the spreading sky

860	Or between the seas, neither south nor north,
	Was there a warrior worthier to rule over men.
	(But no one meant Beowulf's praise to belittle
	Hrothgar, their kind and gracious king!)
	And sometimes, when the path ran straight and
	clear,
865	They would let their horses race, red
	And brown and pale yellow backs streaming
	Down the road. And sometimes a proud old soldier
	Who had heard songs of the ancient heroes
	And could sing them all through, story after story,
870	Would weave a net of words for Beowulf's
	Victory, tying the knot of his verses
	Smoothly, swiftly, into place with a poet's
	Quick skill, singing his new song aloud
	While he shaped it, and the old songs as well—
	Siegmund's
875	Adventures, familiar battles fought
	By that glorious son of Vels. And struggles,
	Too, against evil and treachery that no one
	Had ever heard of, that no one knew
	Except Fitla, who had fought at his uncle's side,
880	A brave young comrade carefully listening
	When Siegmund's tongue unwound the wonders
	He had worked, confiding in his closest friend.
	There were tales of giants wiped from the earth
	By Siegmund's might—and forever remembered,
885	Fame that would last him beyond life and death,
	His daring battle with a treasure-rich dragon.
	Heaving a hoary gray rock aside
	Siegmund had gone down to the dragon alone,
	Entered the hole where it hid and swung
890	His sword so savagely that it slit the creature
	Through, pierced its flesh and pinned it
	To a wall, hung it where his bright blade rested.
	His courage and strength had earned him a kinglike
	Treasure, brought gold and rich rings to his glorious
895	Hands. He loaded that precious hoard
	On his ship and sailed off with a shining cargo.
	And the dragon dissolved in its own fierce blood.
	No prince, no protector of his warriors, knew
	power

And fame and glory like Siegmund's; his name

900 And his treasures grew great. Hermod could have
        hoped
For at least as much; he was once the mightiest
Of men. But pride and defeat and betrayal
Sent him into exile with the Jutes, and he ended
His life on their swords. That life had been misery

905 After misery, and he spread sorrow as long
As he lived it, heaped troubles on his unhappy
        people's
Heads, ignored all wise men's warnings,
Ruled only with courage. A king
Born, entrusted with ancient treasures

910 And cities full of stronghearted soldiers,
His vanity swelled him so vile and rank
That he could hear no voices but his own. He
        deserved
To suffer and die. But Beowulf was a prince
Well-loved, followed in friendship, not fear;

915 Hermod's heart had been hollowed by sin.
        The horses ran, when they could, on the gravel
Path. Morning slid past and was gone.
The whole brave company came riding to Herot,
Anxious to celebrate Beowulf's success

920 And stare at that arm. And Hrothgar rose
From beside his wife and came with his courtiers
Crowded around him. And Welthow rose
And joined him, his wife and queen with her
        women,
All of them walking to that wonderful hall.

14

925   Hrothgar stood at the top of the stairway
And stared at Grendel's great claw, swinging
High from that gold-shining roof. Then he cried:
    "Let God be thanked! Grendel's terrible

Anger hung over our heads too long,
930 Dropping down misery; but the Almighty makes miracles
When He pleases, wonder after wonder, and this world
Rests in His hands. I had given up hope,
Exhausted prayer, expected nothing
But misfortune forever. Herot was empty,
935 Bloody; the wisest and best of our people
Despaired as deeply, found hope no easier,
Knew nothing, no way to end this unequal
War of men and devils, warriors
And monstrous fiends. One man found it,
940 Came to Denmark and with the Lord's help
Did what none of the Danes could do,
Our wisdom, our strength, worthless without him.
The woman who bore him, whoever, wherever,
Alive now, or dead, knew the grace of the God
945 Of our fathers, was granted a son for her glory
And His. Beowulf, best of soldiers,
Let me take you to my heart, make you my son too,
And love you: preserve this passionate peace
Between us. And take, in return, whatever
950 You may want from whatever I own. Warriors
Deserving far less have been granted as much,
Given gifts and honored, though they fought
No enemy like yours. Glory is now yours
Forever and ever, your courage has earned it,
955 And your strength. May God be as good to you forever
As He has been to you here!"
                         Then Beowulf
         answered:
      "What we did was what our hearts helped
Our hands to perform; we came to fight
960 With Grendel, our strength against his. I wish
I could show you, here in Herot, his corpse
Stretched on this floor! I twisted my fingers
Around his claw, ripped and tore at it
As hard as I could: I meant to kill him
965 Right here, hold him so tightly that his heart
Would stop, would break, his life spill

On this floor. But God's will was against me,
As hard as I held him he still pulled free
And ran, escaped from this hall with the strength
970 Fear had given him. But he offered me his arm
And his claw, saved his life yet left me
That prize. And paying even so willingly
For his freedom he still fled with nothing
But the end of his evil days, ran
975 With death pressing at his back, pain
Splitting his panicked heart, pulling him
Step by step into hell. Let him burn
In torment, lying and trembling, waiting
For the brightness of God to bring him his reward."
980   Unferth grew quiet, gave up quarreling over
Beowulf's old battles, stopped all his boasting
Once everyone saw proof of that prince's strength,
Grendel's huge claw swinging high
From Hrothgar's mead-hall roof, the fingers
985 Of that loathsome hand ending in nails
As hard as bright steel—so hard, they all said,
That not even the sharpest of swords could have cut
It through, broken it off the monster's
Arm and ended its life, as Beowulf
990 Had done armed with only his bare hands.

15

Then the king ordered Herot cleaned
And hung with decorations: hundreds of hands,
Men and women, hurried to make
The great hall ready. Golden tapestries
995 Were lined along the walls, for a host
Of visitors to see and take pleasure in. But that
     glorious
building was bent and broken, its iron
Hinges cracked and sprung from their corners
All around the hall. Only

1000   Its roof was undamaged when the blood-stained
        demon
    Burst out of Herot, desperately breaking
    Beowulf's grip, running wildly
    From what no one escapes, struggle and writhe
    As he will. Wanting to stay we go,
1005   All beings here on God's earth, wherever
    It is written that we go, taking our bodies
    From death's cold bed to the unbroken sleep
    That follows life's feast.
                        Then Hrothgar made his way
1010   To the hall; it was time, and his heart drew him
    To the banquet. No victory was celebrated better,
    By more or by better men and their king.
    A mighty host, and famous, they lined
    The benches, rejoicing; the king and Hrothulf,
1015   His nephew, toasted each other, raised mead-cups
    High under Herot's great roof, their speech
    Courteous and warm. King and people
    Were one; none of the Danes was plotting,
    Then, no treachery hid in their smiles.
1020   Healfdane's son gave Beowulf a golden
    Banner, a fitting flag to signal
    His victory, and gave him, as well, a helmet,
    And a coat of mail, and an ancient sword;
    They were brought to him while the warriors
        watched. Beowulf
1025   Drank to those presents, not ashamed to be praised,
    Richly rewarded in front of them all.
    No ring-giver has given four such gifts,
    Passed such treasures through his hands, with the
        grace
    And warmth that Hrothgar showed. The helmet's
1030   Brim was wound with bands of metal,
    Rounded ridges to protect whoever
    Wore it from swords swung in the fiercest
    Battles, shining iron edges
    In hostile hands. And then the protector
1035   Of warriors, lord of the Danes, ordered
    Eight horses led to the hall, and into it,
    Eight steeds with golden bridles. One stood
    With a jeweled saddle on its back, carved

Like the king's war-seat it was; it had carried
1040   Hrothgar when that great son of Healfdane rode
To war—and each time carried him wherever
The fighting was most fierce, and his followers had
    fallen.
Then Beowulf had been honored by both the gifts
Hrothgar could have given him, horses and
    weapons:
1045   The king commanded him to use them well.
Thus that guardian of Denmark's treasures
Had repaid a battle fought for his people
By giving noble gifts, had earned praise
For himself from those who try to know truth.

16

1050   And more: the lord of Herot ordered
Treasure-gifts for each of the Geats
Who'd sailed with Beowulf and still sat beside him,
Ancient armor and swords—and for the one
Murdered by Grendel gold was carefully
1055   Paid. The monster would have murdered again
And again had not God, and the hero's courage,
Turned fate aside. Then and now
Men must lie in their Maker's holy
Hands, moved only as He wills:
1060   Our hearts must seek out that will. The world,
And its long days full of labor, brings good
And evil; all who remain here meet both.
    Hrothgar's hall resounded with the harp's
High call, with songs and laughter and the telling
1065   Of tales, stories sung by the court
Poet as the joyful Danes drank
And listened, seated along their mead-benches.
He told them of Finn's people, attacking
Hnaf with no warning, half wiping out
1070   That Danish tribe, and killing its king.

Finn's wife, Hnaf's sister, learned what good faith
Was worth to her husband: his honeyed words
And treachery cost her two belovèd lives,
Her son and her brother, both falling on spears
1075   Guided by fate's hand. How she wept!
And when morning came she had reason to mourn,
To weep for her dead, her slaughtered son
And the bloody corpse of his uncle—both
The men she most dearly loved, and whose love
1080   She could trust to protect her. But Finn's troops,
        too,
Had fallen to Danish spears: too few
Were left to drive the Danes to their death,
To force Hnaf's follower, Hengest, to flee
The hall where they'd fought and he'd stayed. Finn
        offered them,
1085   Instead of more war, words of peace:
There would be no victory, they'd divide the hall
And the throne, half to the Danes, half
To Finn's followers. When gifts were given
Finn would give Hengest and his soldiers half,
1090   Share shining rings, silver
And gold, with the Danes, both sides equal,
All of them richer, all of their purses
Heavy, every man's heart warm
With the comfort of gold.
1095   Both sides accepted
Peace and agreed to keep it. Finn
Swore it with solemn oaths: what wise men
Had written was his word as well as theirs.
He and the brave Hengest would live
1100   Like brothers; neither leader nor led would break
The truce, would not talk of evil things,
Remind the Danes that the man they served
Killed Hnaf, their lord. They had no king,
And no choice. And he swore that his sword would
        silence
1105   Wagging tongues if Frisian warriors
Stirred up hatred, brought back the past.
    A funeral pyre was prepared, and gold
Was brought; Hnaf's dead body was dressed
For burning, and the others with him. Bloody

1110 Mail shirts could be seen, and golden helmets,
Some carved with boar-heads, all battle-hard
And as useless, now, as the corpses that still wore
    them,
Soldier after soldier! Then Hnaf's sister,
Finn's sad wife, gave her son's body
1115 To be burned in that fire; the flames charring
His uncle would consume both kinsmen at once.
Then she wept again, and weeping sang
The dead's last praise. The Danish king
Was lifted into place, smoke went curling
1120 Up, logs roared, open
wounds split and burst, skulls
Melted, blood came bubbling down,
And the greedy fire-demons drank flesh and bones
From the dead of both sides, until nothing was left.

17

1125   Finn released a few of his soldiers,
Allowed them to return to their distant towns
And estates. Hengest lived the whole stormy
Winter through, there with Finn
Whom he hated. But his heart lived in Denmark—
1130 Which he and the other survivors could not visit,
Could not sail to, as long as the wind-whipped sea
Crashed and whirled, or while winter's cold hands
Froze the water hard, tied it
In icy knots. They would wait for the new year,
1135 For spring to come following the sun, melting
The old year away and reopening the ocean.
Winter was over, the earth grew lovely,
And Hengest dreamed of his home—but revenge
Came first, settling his bitter feud
1140 With Finn, whose bloody sword he could never
Forget. He planned, he waited, wove plans
And waited. Then a Danish warrior dropped

A sword in his lap, a weapon Finn
And his men remembered and feared, and the time
1145   Had come, and Hengest rose, hearing
The Danes' murmur, and drove his new sword
Into Finn's belly, butchering that king
Under his own roof. And the Danes rose,
Their hearts full of Finn's treachery,
1150   And the misery he'd brought them, their sword arms
        restless
And eager. The hall they'd shared with their enemies
Ran red with enemy blood and bodies
Rolled on the floor beside Finn. They took
The queen, looted everything they could find
1155   That belonged to her dead husband, loaded
Their ship with rings, necklaces, shining
Jewels wonderfully worked, and sailed
Bringing treasure and a willing captive to the land
She'd left and had longed for, alone no longer.
1160   The singer finished his song; his listeners
Laughed and drank, their pleasure loud
In that hall. The cup-bearers hurried with their
        sparkling
Vessels. And then the queen, Welthow, wearing her
        bright crown,
Appeared among them, came to Hrothgar and
        Hrothulf, his nephew,
1165   Seated peacefully together, their friendship and
        Hrothulf's good faith still unbroken.
And Unferth sat at Hrothgar's feet; everyone trusted
        him,
Believed in his courage, although he'd spilled his
        relatives' blood.
Then Welthow spoke:
                     "Accept this cup,
1170   My lord and king! May happiness come
To the Danes' great ring-giver; may the Geats receive
Mild words from your mouth, words they have earned!
Let gifts flow freely from your open hands,
Treasures your armies have brought you from all over
1175   The world. I have heard that the greatest of the Geats
Now rests in your heart like a son. Herot
Stands purged, restored by his strength: celebrate

His courage, rejoice and be generous while a kingdom
Sits in your palm, a people and power
1180 That death will steal. But your sons will be safe,
Sheltered in Hrothulf's gracious protection,
If fate takes their father while Hrothulf is alive;
I know your nephew's kindness, I know
He'll repay in kind the goodness you have shown him,
1185 Support your two young sons as you
And I sustained him in his own early days,
His father dead and he but a boy."
    Then she walked to the bench where Hrethric and
      Hrothmund,
Her two sons, sat together; Beowulf,
1190 Prince of the Geats, was seated between them;
Crossing the hall she sat quietly at their side.

18

    They brought a foaming cup and offered it
To Beowulf; it was taken and given in friendship.
And he was given a mail shirt, and golden armbands,
1195 And the most beautiful necklace known to men:
Nowhere in any treasure-hoard anywhere
On earth was there anything like it, not since
Hama carried the Brosings' necklace
Home to his glorious city, saved
1200 Its tight-carved jewels, and his skin, and his soul
From Ermric's treachery, and then came to God.
Higlac had it next, Swerting's
Grandson; defending the golden hoard
His battle-hard hands had won for him, the Geats'
1205 Proud king lost it, was carried away
By fate when too much pride made him feud
With the Frisians. He had asked for misery; it was
    granted him.
He'd borne those precious stones on a ship's
Broad back; he fell beneath his shield.

1210	His body, and his shining coat of mail,
	And that necklace, all lay for Franks to pluck,
	For jackal warriors to find when they walked through
	The rows of corpses; Geats, and their king,
	Lay slaughtered wherever the robbers looked.
1215	The warriors shouted. And Welthow spoke:
	"Wear these bright jewels, belovèd Beowulf;
	Enjoy them, and the rings, and the gold, oh fortunate young
	Warrior; grow richer, let your fame and your strength
	Go hand in hand; and lend these two boys
1220	Your wise and gentle heart! I'll remember your
	Kindness. Your glory is too great to forget:
	It will last forever, wherever the earth
	Is surrounded by the sea, the winds' home,
	And waves lap at its walls. Be happy
1225	For as long as you live! Your good fortune warms
	My soul. Spread your blessèd protection
	Across my son, and my king's son!
	All men speak softly, here, speak mildly
	And trust their neighbors, protect their lord,
1230	Are loyal followers who would fight as joyfully
	As they drink. May your heart help you do as I ask!"
	She returned to her seat. The soldiers ate
	And drank like kings. The savage fate
	Decreed for them hung dark and unknown, what would follow
1235	After nightfall, when Hrothgar withdrew from the hall,
	Sought his bed and left his soldiers
	To theirs. Herot would house a host
	Of men, that night, as it had been meant to do.
	They stacked away the benches, spread out
1240	Blankets and pillows. But those beer-drinking sleepers
	Lay down with death beside their beds.
	They slept with their shining shields at the edge
	Of their pillows; the hall was filled with helmets
	Hanging near motionless heads; spears
1245	Stood by their hands, their hammered mail shirts
	Covered their chests. It was the Danes' custom
	To be ready for war, wherever they rested,

At home or in foreign lands, at their lord's
Quick call if he needed them, if trouble came
1250   To their king. They knew how soldiers must live!

19

They sank into sleep. The price of that evening's
Rest was too high for the Dane who bought it
With his life, paying as others had paid
When Grendel inhabited Herot, the hall
1255   His till his crimes pulled him into hell.
And now it was known that a monster had died
But a monster still lived, and meant revenge.
She'd brooded on her loss, misery had brewed
In her heart, that female horror, Grendel's
1260   Mother, living in the murky cold lake
Assigned her since Cain had killed his only
Brother, slain his father's son
With an angry sword. God drove him off,
Outlawed him to the dry and barren desert,
1265   And branded him with a murderer's mark. And he
        bore
A race of fiends accursed like their father;
So Grendel was drawn to Herot, an outcast
Come to meet the man who awaited him.
He'd snatched at Beowulf's arm, but that prince
1270   Remembered God's grace and the strength He'd given
        him
And relied on the Lord for all the help,
The comfort and support he would need. He killed
The monster, as God had meant him to do,
Tore the fiend apart and forced him
1275   To run as rapidly as he could toward death's
Cold waiting hands. His mother's sad heart,
And her greed, drove her from her den on the
        dangerous

Pathway of revenge.

So she reached Herot,
1280   Where the Danes slept as though already dead;
Her visit ended their good fortune, reversed
The bright vane of their luck. No female, no matter
How fierce, could have come with a man's strength,
Fought with the power and courage men fight with,
1285   Smashing their shining swords, their bloody,
Hammer-forged blades onto boar-headed helmets,
Slashing and stabbing with the sharpest of points.
The soldiers raised their shields and drew
Those gleaming swords, swung them above
1290   The piled-up benches, leaving their mail shirts
And their helmets where they'd lain when the terror
    took hold of them.
To save her life she moved still faster,
Took a single victim and fled from the hall,
Running to the moors, discovered, but her supper
1295   Assured, sheltered in her dripping claws.
She'd taken Hrothgar's closest friend,
The man he most loved of all men on earth;
She'd killed a glorious soldier, cut
A noble life short. No Geat could have stopped her:
1300   Beowulf and his band had been given better
Beds; sleep had come to them in a different
Hall. Then all Herot burst into shouts:
She had carried off Grendel's claw. Sorrow
Had returned to Denmark. They'd traded deaths,
1305   Danes and monsters, and no one had won,
Both had lost!

The wise old king
Trembled in anger and grief, his dearest
Friend and adviser dead. Beowulf
1310   Was sent for at once: a messenger went swiftly
To his rooms and brought him. He came, his band
About him, as dawn was breaking through,
The best of all warriors, walking to where Hrothgar
Sat waiting, the gray-haired king wondering
1315   If God would ever end this misery.
The Geats tramped quickly through the hall; their
    steps
Beat and echoed in the silence. Beowulf

Rehearsed the words he would want with Hrothgar;
He'd ask the Danes' great lord if all
1320   Were at peace, if the night had passed quietly.

20

Hrothgar answered him, protector of his people:
"There's no happiness to ask about! Anguish has
    descended
On the Danes. Esher is dead, Ermlaf's
Older brother and my own most trusted
1325   Counselor and friend, my comrade, when we went
Into battle, who'd beaten back enemy swords,
Standing at my side. All my soldiers
Should be as he was, their hearts as brave
And as wise! Another wandering fiend
1330   Has found him in Herot, murdered him, fled
With his corpse: he'll be eaten, his flesh become
A horrible feast—and who knows where
The beast may be hiding, its belly stuffed full?
She's taking revenge for your victory over Grendel,
1335   For your strength, your mighty grip, and that
        monster's
Death. For years he'd been preying on my people;
You came, he was dead in a single day,
And now there's another one, a second hungry
Fiend, determined to avenge the first,
1340   A monster willing and more than able
To bring us more sorrow—or so it must seem
To the many men mourning that noble
Treasure-giver, for all men were treated
Nobly by those hands now forever closed.
1345   "I've heard that my people, peasants working
In the fields, have seen a pair of such fiends
Wandering in the moors and marshes, giant
Monsters living in those desert lands.

And they've said to my wise men that, as well as they
    could see,
1350   One of the devils was a female creature.
The other, they say, walked through the wilderness
Like a man—but mightier than any man.
They were frightened, and they fled, hoping to find
    help
In Herot. They named the huge one Grendel:
1355   If he had a father no one knew him,
Or whether there'd been others before these two,
Hidden evil before hidden evil.
They live in secret places, windy
Cliffs, wolf-dens where water pours
1360   From the rocks, then runs underground, where mist
Steams like black clouds, and the groves of trees
Growing out over their lake are all covered
With frozen spray, and wind down snakelike
Roots that reach as far as the water
1365   And help keep it dark. At night that lake
Burns like a torch. No one knows its bottom,
No wisdom reaches such depths. A deer,
Hunted through the woods by packs of hounds,
A stag with great horns, though driven through the
    forest
1370   From faraway places, prefers to die
On those shores, refuses to save its life
In that water. It isn't far, nor is it
A pleasant spot! When the wind stirs
And storms, waves splash toward the sky,
1375   As dark as the air, as black as the rain
That the heavens weep. Our only help,
Again, lies with you. Grendel's mother
Is hidden in her terrible home, in a place
You've not seen. Seek it, if you dare! Save us,
1380   Once more, and again twisted gold,
Heaped-up ancient treasure, will reward you
For the battle you win!"

Beowulf spoke:
"Let your sorrow end! It is better for us all
1385   To avenge our friends, not mourn them forever.
Each of us will come to the end of this life
On earth; he who can earn it should fight
For the glory of his name; fame after death
Is the noblest of goals. Arise, guardian
1390   Of this kingdom, let us go, as quickly as we can,
And have a look at this lady monster.
I promise you this: she'll find no shelter,
No hole in the ground, no towering tree,
No deep bottom of a lake, where her sins can hide.
1395   Be patient for one more day of misery;
I ask for no longer."
                 The old king leaped
To his feet, gave thanks to God for such words.
Then Hrothgar's horse was brought, saddled
1400   And bridled. The Danes' wise ruler rode,
Stately and splendid; shield-bearing soldiers
Marched at his side. The monster's tracks
Led them through the forest; they followed her heavy
Feet, that had swept straight across
1405   The shadowy waste land, her burden the lifeless
Body of the best of Hrothgar's men.
The trail took them up towering, rocky
Hills, and over narrow, winding
Paths they had never seen, down steep
1410   And slippery cliffs where creatures from deep
In the earth hid in their holes. Hrothgar
Rode in front, with a few of his most knowing
Men, to find their way. Then suddenly,
Where clumps of trees bent across
1415   Cold gray stones, they came to a dismal
Wood; below them was the lake, its water
Bloody and bubbling. And the Danes shivered,
Miserable, mighty men tormented
By grief, seeing, there on that cliff
1420   Above the water, Esher's bloody
Head. They looked down at the lake, felt
How its heat rose up, watched the waves'

Blood-stained swirling. Their battle horns sounded,
Then sounded again. Then they set down their
    weapons.

1425   They could see the water crawling with snakes,
Fantastic serpents swimming in the boiling
Lake, and sea beasts lying on the rocks
—The kind that infest the ocean, in the early
Dawn, often ending some ship's

1430   Journey with their wild jaws. They rushed
Angrily out of sight, when the battle horns blew.
Beowulf aimed an arrow at one
Of the beasts, swimming sluggishly away,
And the point pierced its hide, stabbed

1435   To its heart; its life leaked out, death
Swept it off. Quickly, before
The dying monster could escape, they hooked
Its thrashing body with their curved boar-spears,
Fought it to land, drew it up on the bluff,

1440   Then stood and stared at the incredible wave-roamer,
Covered with strange scales and horrible. Then
      Beowulf
Began to fasten on his armor,
Not afraid for his life but knowing the woven
Mail, with its hammered links, could save

1445   That life when he lowered himself into the lake,
Keep slimy monsters' claws from snatching at
His heart, preserve him for the battle he was sent
To fight. Hrothgar's helmet would defend him;
That ancient, shining treasure, encircled

1450   With hard-rolled metal, set there by some smith's
Long dead hand, would block all battle
Swords, stop all blades from cutting at him
When he'd swum toward the bottom, gone down in
      the surging
Water, deep toward the swirling sands.

1455   And Unferth helped him, Hrothgar's courtier
Lent him a famous weapon, a fine,
Hilted old sword named Hrunting; it had
An iron blade, etched and shining
And hardened in blood. No one who'd worn it

1460   Into battle, swung it in dangerous places,
Daring and brave, had ever been deserted—

Nor was Beowulf's journey the first time it was taken
To an enemy's camp, or asked to support
Some hero's courage and win him glory.
1465 Unferth had tried to forget his greeting
To Beowulf, his drunken speech of welcome;
A mighty warrior, he lent his weapon
To a better one. Only Beowulf would risk
His life in that lake; Unferth was afraid,
1470 Gave up that chance to work wonders, win glory
And a hero's fame. But Beowulf and fear
Were strangers; he stood ready to dive into battle.

22

Then Edgetho's brave son spoke:
                                        "Remember,
1475 Hrothgar, Oh knowing king, now
When my danger is near, the warm words we uttered,
And if your enemy should end my life
Then be, oh generous prince, forever
The father and protector of all whom I leave
1480 Behind me, here in your hands, my belovèd
Comrades left with no leader, their leader
Dead. And the precious gifts you gave me,
My friend, send them to Higlac. May he see
In their golden brightness, the Geats' great lord
1485 Gazing at your treasure, that here in Denmark
I found a noble protector, a giver
Of rings whose rewards I won and briefly
Relished. And you, Unferth, let
My famous old sword stay in your hands:
1490 I shall shape glory with Hrunting, or death
Will hurry me from this earth!"
                                        As his words ended
He leaped into the lake, would not wait for anyone's
Answer; the heaving water covered him
1495 Over. For hours he sank through the waves;

At last he saw the mud of the bottom.
And all at once the greedy she-wolf
Who'd ruled those waters for half a hundred
Years discovered him, saw that a creature
1500 From above had come to explore the bottom
Of her wet world. She welcomed him in her claws,
Clutched at him savagely but could not harm him,
Tried to work her fingers through the tight
Ring-woven mail on his breast, but tore
1505 And scratched in vain. Then she carried him, armor
And sword and all, to her home; he struggled
To free his weapon, and failed. The fight
Brought other monsters swimming to see
Her catch, a host of sea beasts who beat at
1510 His mail shirt, stabbing with tusks and teeth
As they followed along. Then he realized, suddenly,
That she'd brought him into someone's battle-hall,
And there the water's heat could not hurt him,
Nor anything in the lake attack him through
1515 The building's high-arching roof. A brilliant
Light burned all around him, the lake
Itself like a fiery flame.
                                                    Then he saw
The mighty water witch, and swung his sword,
1520 His ring-marked blade, straight at her head;
The iron sang its fierce song,
Sang Beowulf's strength. But her guest
Discovered that no sword could slice her evil
Skin, that Hrunting could not hurt her, was useless
1525 Now when he needed it. They wrestled, she ripped
And tore and clawed at him, bit holes in his helmet,
And that too failed him; for the first time in years
Of being worn to war it would earn no glory;
It was the last time anyone would wear it. But Beowulf
1530 Longed only for fame, leaped back
Into battle. He tossed his sword aside,
Angry; the steel-edged blade lay where
He'd dropped it. If weapons were useless he'd use
His hands, the strength in his fingers. So fame
1535 Comes to the men who mean to win it
And care about nothing else! He raised
His arms and seized her by the shoulder; anger

Doubled his strength, he threw her to the floor.
She fell, Grendel's fierce mother, and the Geats'
1540   Proud prince was ready to leap on her. But she rose
At once and repaid him with her clutching claws,
Wildly tearing at him. He was weary, that best
And strongest of soldiers; his feet stumbled
And in an instant she had him down, held helpless.
1545   Squatting with her weight on his stomach, she drew
A dagger, brown with dried blood, and prepared
To avenge her only son. But he was stretched
On his back, and her stabbing blade was blunted
By the woven mail shirt he wore on his chest.
1550   The hammered links held; the point
Could not touch him. He'd have traveled to the
        bottom of the earth,
Edgetho's son, and died there, if that shining
Woven metal had not helped—and Holy
God, who sent him victory, gave judgment
1555   For truth and right, Ruler of the Heavens,
Once Beowulf was back on his feet and fighting.

23

Then he saw, hanging on the wall, a heavy
Sword, hammered by giants, strong
And blessed with their magic, the best of all weapons
1560   But so massive that no ordinary man could lift
Its carved and decorated length. He drew it
From its scabbard, broke the chain on its hilt,
And then, savage, now, angry
And desperate, lifted it high over his head
1565   And struck with all the strength he had left,
Caught her in the neck and cut it through,
Broke bones and all. Her body fell
To the floor, lifeless, the sword was wet
With her blood, and Beowulf rejoiced at the sight.
1570   The brilliant light shone, suddenly,

As though burning in that hall, and as bright as
    Heaven's
Own candle, lit in the sky. He looked
At her home, then following along the wall
Went walking, his hands tight on the sword,
1575 His heart still angry. He was hunting another
Dead monster, and took his weapon with him
For final revenge against Grendel's vicious
Attacks, his nighttime raids, over
And over, coming to Herot when Hrothgar's
1580 Men slept, killing them in their beds,
Eating some on the spot, fifteen
Or more, and running to his loathsome moor
With another such sickening meal waiting
In his pouch. But Beowulf repaid him for those visits,
1585 Found him lying dead in his corner,
Armless, exactly as that fierce fighter
Had sent him out from Herot, then struck off
His head with a single swift blow. The body
Jerked for the last time, then lay still.
1590   The wise old warriors who surrounded Hrothgar,
Like him staring into the monsters' lake,
Saw the waves surging and blood
Spurting through. They spoke about Beowulf,
All the graybeards, whispered together
1595 And said that hope was gone, that the hero
Had lost fame and his life at once, and would never
Return to the living, come back as triumphant
As he had left; almost all agreed that Grendel's
Mighty mother, the she-wolf, had killed him.
1600 The sun slid over past noon, went further
Down. The Danes gave up, left
The lake and went home, Hrothgar with them.
The Geats stayed, sat sadly, watching,
Imagining they saw their lord but not believing
They would ever see him again.
1605   —Then the sword
Melted, blood-soaked, dripping down
Like water, disappearing like ice when the world's
Eternal Lord loosens invisible
Fetters and unwinds icicles and frost
1610 As only He can, He who rules

Time and seasons, He who is truly
God. The monsters' hall was full of
Rich treasures, but all that Beowulf took
Was Grendel's head and the hilt of the giants'
1615 Jeweled sword; the rest of that ring-marked
Blade had dissolved in Grendel's steaming
Blood, boiling even after his death.
And then the battle's only survivor
Swam up and away from those silent corpses;
1620 The water was calm and clean, the whole
Huge lake peaceful once the demons who'd lived in it
Were dead.
              Then that noble protector of all seamen
Swam to land, rejoicing in the heavy
1625 Burdens he was bringing with him. He
And all his glorious band of Geats
Thanked God that their leader had come back
      unharmed;
They left the lake together. The Geats
Carried Beowulf's helmet, and his mail shirt.
1630 Behind them the water slowly thickened
As the monsters' blood came seeping up.
They walked quickly, happily, across
Roads all of them remembered, left
The lake and the cliffs alongside it, brave men
1635 Staggering under the weight of Grendel's skull,
Too heavy for fewer than four of them to handle—
Two on each side of the spear jammed through it—
Yet proud of their ugly load and determined
That the Danes, seated in Herot, should see it.
1640 Soon, fourteen Geats arrived
At the hall, bold and warlike, and with Beowulf,
Their lord and leader, they walked on the mead-hall
Green. Then the Geats' brave prince entered
Herot, covered with glory for the daring
1645 Battles he had fought; he sought Hrothgar
To salute him and show Grendel's head.
He carried that terrible trophy by the hair,
Brought it straight to where the Danes sat,
Drinking, the queen among them. It was a weird
1650 And wonderful sight, and the warriors stared.

24

Beowulf spoke:
"Hrothgar! Behold,
Great Healfdane's son, this glorious sign
Of victory, brought you by joyful Geats.
1655 My life was almost lost, fighting for it,
Struggling under water: I'd have been dead at once,
And the fight finished, the she-devil victorious,
If our Father in Heaven had not helped me. Hrunting,
Unferth's noble weapon, could do nothing,
1660 Nor could I, until the ruler of the world
Showed me, hanging shining and beautiful
On a wall, a mighty old sword—so God
Gives guidance to those who can find it from no one
Else. I used the weapon He had offered me,
1665 Drew it and, when I could, swung it, killed
The monstrous hag in her own home.
Then the ring-marked blade burned away,
As that boiling blood spilled out. I carried
Off all that was left, this hilt.
1670 I've avenged their crimes, and the Danes they've
killed.
And I promise you that whoever sleeps in Herot
—You, your brave soldiers, anyone
Of all the people in Denmark, old
Or young—they, and you, may now sleep
1675 Without fear of either monster, mother
Or son."
Then he gave the golden sword hilt
To Hrothgar, who held it in his wrinkled hands
And stared at what giants had made, and monsters
1680 Owned; it was his, an ancient weapon
Shaped by wonderful smiths, now that Grendel
And his evil mother had been driven from the earth,
God's enemies scattered and dead. That best
Of swords belonged to the best of Denmark's
1685 Rulers, the wisest ring-giver Danish
Warriors had ever known. The old king
Bent close to the handle of the ancient relic,
And saw written there the story of ancient wars
Between good and evil, the opening of the waters,

1690   The Flood sweeping giants away, how they suffered
And died, that race who hated the Ruler
Of us all and received judgment from His hands,
Surging waves that found them wherever
They fled. And Hrothgar saw runic letters
1695   Clearly carved in that shining hilt,
Spelling its original owner's name,
He for whom it was made, with its twisted
Handle and snakelike carvings. Then he spoke,
Healfdane's son, and everyone was silent.

1700   "What I say, speaking from a full memory
And after a life spent in seeking
What was right for my people, is this: this prince
Of the Geats, Beowulf, was born a better
Man! Your fame is everywhere, my friend,
1705   Reaches to the ends of the earth, and you hold it in
        your heart wisely,
Patient with your strength and our weakness. What I
        said I will do, I will do,
In the name of the friendship we've sworn. Your
        strength must solace your people,
Now, and mine no longer.
                    "Be not
1710   As Hermod once was to my people, too proud
To care what their hearts hid, bringing them
Only destruction and slaughter. In his mad
Rages he killed them himself, comrades
And followers who ate at his table. At the end
1715   He was alone, knew none of the joys of life
With other men, a famous ruler
Granted greater strength than anyone
Alive in his day but dark and bloodthirsty
In spirit. He shared out no treasure, showed
1720   His soldiers no road to riches and fame.
And then that affliction on his people's face
Suffered horribly for his sins. Be taught
By his lesson, learn what a king must be:
I tell his tale, old as I am,
1725   Only for you.
                "Our eternal Lord
Grants some men wisdom, some wealth, makes others
Great. The world is God's, He allows

A man to grow famous, and his family rich,
1730 Gives him land and towns to rule
And delight in, lets his kingdom reach
As far as the world runs—and who
In human unwisdom, in the middle of such power,
Remembers that it all will end, and too soon?
1735 Prosperity, prosperity, prosperity: nothing
Troubles him, no sickness, not passing time,
No sorrows, no sudden war breaking
Out of nowhere, but all the world turns
When he spins it. How can he know when he sins?

25

1740   "And then pride grows in his heart, planted
Quietly but flourishing. And while the keeper of his
    soul
Sleeps on, while conscience rests and the world
Turns faster a murderer creeps closer, comes carrying
A tight-strung bow with terrible arrows.
1745 And those sharp points strike home, are shot
In his breast, under his helmet. He's helpless.
And so the Devil's dark urgings wound him, for he
    can't
Remember how he clung to the rotting wealth
Of this world, how he clawed to keep it, how he
    earned
1750 No honor, no glory, in giving golden
Rings, how he forgot the future glory
God gave him at his birth, and forgetting did not care.
And finally his body fails him, these bones
And flesh quickened by God fall
1755 And die—and some other soul inherits
His place in Heaven, some open-handed
Giver of old treasures, who takes no delight
In mere gold. Guard against such wickedness,
Belovèd Beowulf, best of warriors,

1760 And choose, instead, eternal happiness;
Push away pride! Your strength, your power,
Are yours for how many years? Soon
You'll return them where they came from, sickness or
     a sword's edge
Will end them, or a grasping fire, or the flight
1765 Of a spear, or surging waves, or a knife's
Bite, or the terror of old age, or your eyes
Darkening over. It will come, death
Comes faster than you think, no one can flee it.
     "So I have led the Danes for half
1770 A hundred years, protected them from all peoples
On this earth, my sword and my spear so ready
That no one anywhere under God's high sun
Was eager to wage war here in Denmark.
And here, here too the change has come,
1775 And we wept for our dead when Grendel invaded
Herot, my enemy raided this hall;
My sorrow, my grief, was as great and lasting
As it was helpless. Then thanks be given to God,
Eternal Lord of us all: you came
1780 And that endless misery was over and I lived,
Now, to behold this bloody head!
Go in, go in: feast, be as happy
As your fame deserves. When morning shines
We shall each have owned more of my treasures."
1785   Beowulf obeyed him, entered Herot
Cheerfully and took his place at the table.
And once again Danes and Geats
Feasted together, a host of famous
Warriors in a single hall.—Then the web
1790 Of darkness fell and it was night. They rose;
Hrothgar, the gray-haired old Dane, was heavy
With sleep. And Beowulf was glad that a bed
Was waiting, the bravest of warriors exhausted
With the work he'd done. A Danish servant
1795 Showed him the road to that far-off, quiet
Country where sleep would come and take him
And his followers; Hrothgar's visitors were well
Cared for, whatever they needed was theirs.
     Then Beowulf rested; Herot rose high
1800 Above him, gleaming in the darkness; the Geats

Slept till a black-feathered raven sang
His cheerful song and the shining sun
Burned away shadows. And those seafarers hurried
From their beds, anxious to begin the voyage
1805   Home, ready to start, their hearts
Already sailing on a ship's swift back.
        Then Unferth came, with Hrunting, his famous
Sword, and offered it to Beowulf, asked him
To accept a precious gift. The prince
1810   Took it, thanked him, and declared the weapon
One he was proud to own; his words
Blamed it for nothing, were spoken like the hero
He was! The war-gear was ready, the Geats
Were armored and eager to be gone. Quickly,
1815   Beowulf sought Hrothgar's throne, where the king
Sat waiting for his famous visitor's farewell.

26

Beowulf spoke:
                    "We crossed the sea
To come here; it is time to return, to go back
1820   To our belovèd lord, Higlac. Denmark
Was a gracious host; you welcomed us warmly.
Anything I can do, here on this earth,
To earn your love, oh great king, anything
More than I have done, battles I can fight
1825   In your honor, summon me, I will come as I came
Once before. If I hear, from across the ocean,
That your neighbors have threatened you with war, or
        oppressed you
As enemies once oppressed you, here, I will bring
A thousand warriors, a thousand armed Geats
1830   To protect your throne. I trust Higlac:
Our king is young, but if I need his help
To better help you, to lend you our strength,
Our battle-sharp spears, to shield you and honor you

As you deserve, I know his words and his deeds
1835 Will support me. And someday, if your oldest son,
Hrethric, comes visiting our court, he will find
A host of good friends among the Geats:
No one who goes visiting far-off lands
Is more welcome than a strong and noble warrior."
1840 Hrothgar replied:
       "All-knowing God
Must have sent you such words; nothing so wise
From a warrior so young has ever reached
These ancient ears. Your hands are strong,
1845 Your heart and your lips are knowing! If your lord,
Hrethel's son, is slain by a spear,
Or falls sick and dies, or is killed by a sword,
And you have survived whatever battle
Sweeps him off, I say that the Geats
1850 Could do no better, find no man better
Suited to be king, keeper of warriors
And their treasure, than you—if you take the throne
They will surely offer you. Belovèd Beowulf,
You please me more the longer I can keep you
1855 Here in Denmark. You've turned Danes
And Geats into brothers, brought peace where once
There was war, and sealed friendship with affection.
This will last as long as I live, and am king here:
We will share our treasures, greeting travelers
1860 From across the sea with outstretched hands;
Ring-prowed ships will carry our gifts
And the tokens of our love. Your people live
By the old ways, their hearts, like ours, are forever
Open to their friends, but firmly closed
1865 Against their enemies."
         Then he gave the Geats'
Prince a dozen new gifts, prayed
For his safety, commanded him to seek his people,
Yet not to delay too long in visiting
1870 Hrothgar once more. The old king kissed him,
Held that best of all warriors by the shoulder
And wept, unable to hold back his tears.
Gray and wise, he knew how slim
Were his chances of ever greeting Beowulf
1875 Again, but seeing his face he was forced

To hope. His love was too warm to be hidden,
His tears came running too quickly to be checked;
His very blood burned with longing.
And then Beowulf left him, left Herot, walked
1880 Across the green in his golden armor,
Exulting in the treasures heaped high in his arms.
His ship was at anchor; he had it ready to sail.
And so Hrothgar's rich treasures would leave him,
 travel
Far from that perfect king, without fault
1885 Or blame until winter had followed winter
And age had stolen his strength, spirited it
Off, as it steals from many men.

27

Then the band of Geats, young and brave,
Marching in their ring-locked armor, reached
1890 The shore. The coast-guard saw them coming
And about to go as he'd seen them before;
He hurried down the hillside, whipping
His horse, but this time shouted no challenge,
Told them only how the Geats would be watching
1895 Too, and would welcome such warriors in shining
Mail. Their broad-beamed ship lay bobbing
At the edge of the sand: they loaded it high
With armor and horses and all the rich treasure
It could hold. The mast stood high and straight
1900 Over heaped-up wealth—Hrothgar's, and now theirs.
Beowulf rewarded the boat's watchman,
Who had stayed behind, with a sword that had
 hammered
Gold wound on its handle: the weapon
Brought him honor. Then the ship left shore, left
 Denmark,
1905 Traveled through deep water. Deck timbers creaked,
And the wind billowing through the sail stretched

From the mast, tied tight with ropes, did not hold
    them
Back, did not keep the ring-prowed ship
From foaming swiftly through the waves, the sea
1910   Currents, across the wide ocean until
They could see familiar headlands, cliffs
That sprang out of Geatish soil. Driven
By the wind the ship rammed high on the shore.
Harbor guards came running to greet them,
1915   Men who for days had waited and watched
For their belovèd comrades to come crossing the
    waves;
They anchored the high-bowed ship, moored it
Close to the shore, where the booming sea
Could not pull it loose and lead it away.
1920   Then they carried up the golden armor,
The ancient swords, the jewels, brought them
To Higlac's home, their ring-giver's hall
Near the sea, where he lived surrounded
By his followers.
1925   He was a famous king, with a fitting
High hall and a wife, Higd, young
But wise and knowing beyond her years.
She was Hareth's daughter, a noble queen
With none of the niggardly ways of women
1930   Like Thrith. Higd gave the Geats gifts
With open hands. But Thrith was too proud,
An imperious princess with a vicious tongue
And so fierce and wild that her father's followers
Averted their eyes as she passed, knowing
1935   That if anyone but their king watched where she
    walked
Her hands would shape a noose to fit
Their necks. She would lie, her father's lieutenants
Would write out her warrants, and he who had stared
Would end his life on the edge of an ancient
1940   Sword. And how great a sin for a woman,
Whether fair or black, to create fear
And destruction, for a woman, who should walk in
    the ways
Of peace, to kill with pretended insults.
But Hemming's kinsman tamed her: his hall-guests

1945   Told a different story, spread the news
That Thrith had forgotten her gory tricks
Once her wise father had sent her to a wedding
With Offa, married her to that brave young soldier,
Sent her across the yellow-green sea
1950   To that gold-adorned champion, a fierce fighter
In war or peace. They praised her, now,
For her generous heart, and her goodness, and the
      high
And most noble paths she walked, filled
With adoring love for that leader of warriors,
1955   Her husband; he was a man as brave and strong
And good, it is said, as anyone on this earth,
A spear-bold soldier who knew no fear,
Exalted with gifts, victorious in war,
A king who ruled his native land
1960   Wisely and well. Emer was his son,
Hemming's kinsman, Garmund's grandson,
A powerful swordsman and his warriors' shield.

28

     Then Beowulf and his men went walking along
The shore, down the broad strip of sand.
1965   The world's bright candle shone, hurrying
Up from the south. It was a short journey
From their ship to Higlac's home, to the hall
Where their king, Ongentho's killer, lived
With his warriors and gave treasures away. They
      walked
1970   Quickly. The young king knew
They were back, Beowulf and his handful of brave
Men, come safely home; he sat,
Now, waiting to see them, to greet
His battle-comrades when they arrived at his court.
1975   They came. And when Beowulf had bowed to his
      lord,

And standing in front of the throne had solemnly
Spoken loyal words, Higlac
Ordered him to sit at his side—he
Who had survived, sailed home victorious, next to
His kinsman and king. Mead cups were filled
And Hareth's daughter took them through the hall,
Carried ale to her husband's comrades.
Higlac, unable to stay silent, anxious
To know how Beowulf's adventure had gone,
Began to question him, courteous but eager
To be told everything.

              "Belovèd Beowulf,
Tell us what your trip to far-off places
Brought you, your sudden expedition on the salty
Waves, your search for war in Herot?
Did you end Hrothgar's hopeless misery,
Could you help that glorious king? Grendel's
Savagery lay heavy on my heart but I was afraid
To let you go to him; for a long time
I held you here, kept you safe,
Forced you to make the Danes fight
Their own battles. God be praised
That my eyes have beheld you once more,
    unharmed!"

    Beowulf spoke, Edgetho's brave son:
    "My lord Higlac, my meeting with Grendel
And the nighttime battle we fought are known
To everyone in Denmark, where the monster was
    once
The uncrowned ruler, murdering and eating
Hrothgar's people, forever bringing them
Misery. I ended his reign, avenged
His crimes so completely in the crashing darkness
That not even the oldest of his evil kind
Will ever boast, lying in sin
And deceit, that the monster beat me. I sought out
Hrothgar, first, came to him in his hall;
When Healfdane's famous son heard
That I'd come to challenge Grendel, he gave me
A seat of honor alongside his son.
His followers were drinking; I joined their feast,
Sat with that band, as bright and loud-tongued

Line numbers (left margin): 1980, 1985, 1990, 1995, 2000, 2005, 2010, 2015

As any I've ever seen. His famous
Queen went back and forth, hurrying
The cup-bearing boys, giving bracelets
And rings to her husband's warriors. I heard
2020   The oldest soldiers of all calling
For ale from Hrothgar's daughter's hands,
And Freaw was the way they greeted her when she
       gave them
The golden cups. And Hrothgar will give her
To Ingeld, gracious Froda's son;
2025   She and that ripening soldier will be married,
The Danes' great lord and protector has declared,
Hoping that his quarrel with the Hathobards can
       be settled
By a woman. He's wrong: how many wars
Have been put to rest in a prince's bed?
2030   Few. A bride can bring a little
Peace, make spears silent for a time,
But not long. Ingeld and all his men
Will be drinking in the hall, when the wedding is
       done
And Freaw is his wife; the Danes will be wearing
2035   Gleaming armor and ring-marked old swords;
And the prince and his people will remember those
       treasures,
Will remember that their fathers once wore them, fell
With those helmets on their heads, those swords in
       their hands.

29

"And seeing their ancestral armor and weapons
2040   Ingeld and his followers will be angry. And one
Of his soldiers, sitting with ale in his cup
And bitterness heavy in his heart, will remember
War and death, and while he sits and drinks
His sharp old tongue will begin to tempt

2045 Some younger warrior, pushing and probing
   For a new war:
         " 'That sword, that precious old blade
   Over there, I think you know it, friend.
   Your father carried it, fought with it the last time
2050 He could swing a sword; the Danes killed him
   —And many more of our men—and stripped
   The dead bodies: the brave, bold Danes!
   One of the princess' people, here,
   Now, might be the murderer's son,
2055 Boasting about his treasures, his ancient
   Armor—which ought to be yours, by right.'
    "Bitter words will work in a hot-tempered
   Brain, pushing up thoughts of the past,
   And then, when he can, calling his father's
2060 Name, the youngster will kill some innocent
   Dane, a servant—and bloody sword
   In hand will run from the hall, knowing
   His way through the woods. But war will begin
   As he runs, to the sound of broken oaths,
2065 And its heat will dry up Ingeld's heart,
   Leave him indifferent to his Danish bride.
   Hrothgar may think the Hathobards love him,
   Loving Freaw, but the friendship can't last,
   The vows are worthless.
2070   "But of Grendel: you need to
   Know more to know everything; I ought to
   Go on. It was early in the evening, Heaven's
   Jewel had slid to its rest, and the jealous
   Monster, planning murder, came seeking us
2075 Out, stalking us as we guarded Hrothgar's
   Hall. Hondshew, sleeping in his armor,
   Was the first Geat he reached: Grendel
   Seized him, tore him apart, swallowed him
   Down, feet and all, as fate
2080 Had decreed—a glorious young soldier, killed
   In his prime. Yet Grendel had only begun
   His bloody work, meant to leave us
   With his belly and his pouch both full, and Herot
   Half-empty. Then he tested his strength against mine,
2085 Hand to hand. His pouch hung
   At his side, a huge bag sewn

From a dragon's skin, worked with a devil's
Skill; it was closed by a marvelous clasp.
The monster intended to take me, put me
2090 Inside, save me for another meal.
He was bold and strong, but once I stood
On my feet his strength was useless, and it failed him.

30

"The whole tale of how I killed him,
Repaid him in kind for all the evil
2095 He'd done, would take too long: your people,
My prince, were honored in the doing. He escaped,
Found a few minutes of life, but his hand,
His whole right arm, stayed in Herot;
The miserable creature crept away,
2100 Dropped to the bottom of his lake, half dead
As he fell. When the sun had returned, the Danes'
Great king poured out treasure, repaid me
In hammered gold for the bloody battle
I'd fought in his name. He ordered a feast;
2105 There were songs, and the telling of tales. One
     ancient
Dane told of long-dead times,
And sometimes Hrothgar himself, with the harp
In his lap, stroked its silvery strings
And told wonderful stories, a brave king
2110 Reciting unhappy truths about good
And evil—and sometimes he wove his stories
On the mournful thread of old age, remembering
Buried strength and the battles it had won.
He would weep, the old king, wise with many
2115 Winters, remembering what he'd done, once,
What he'd seen, what he knew. And so we sat
The day away, feasting. Then darkness
Fell again, and Grendel's mother
Was waiting, ready for revenge, hating

2120 The Danes for her son's death. The monstrous
Hag succeeded, burst boldly into Herot
And killed Esher, one of the king's oldest
And wisest soldiers. But when the sun shone
Once more the death-weary Danes could not build

2125 A pyre and burn his belovèd body,
Lay him on flaming logs, return ashes
To dust: she'd carried away his corpse,
Brought it to her den deep in the water.
Hrothgar had wept for many of his men,

2130 But this time his heart melted, this
Was the worst. He begged me, in your name, half-
weeping
As he spoke, to seek still greater glory
Deep in the swirling waves, to win
Still higher fame, and the gifts he would give me.

2135 Down in that surging lake I sought
And found her, the horrible hag, fierce
And wild; we fought, clutching and grasping;
The water ran red with blood and at last,
With a mighty sword that had hung on the wall,

2140 I cut off her head. I had barely escaped
With my life, my death was not written. And the
Danes'
Protector, Healfdane's great son, heaped up
Treasures and precious jewels to reward me.

31

"He lived his life as a good king must:
2145 I lost nothing, none of the gifts
My strength could have earned me. He opened his
store
Of gems and armor, let me choose as I liked,
So I could bring his riches to you, my ruler,
And prove his friendship, and my love. Your favor

2150 Still governs my life: I have almost no family,

Higlac, almost no one, now, but you."
  Then Beowulf ordered them to bring in the boar-
    head
Banner, the towering helmet, the ancient,
Silvery armor, and the gold-carved sword:
2155 "This war-gear was Hrothgar's reward, my gift
From his wise old hands. He wanted me to tell you,
First, whose treasures these were. Hergar
Had owned them, his older brother, who was king
Of Denmark until death gave Hrothgar the throne:
2160 But Hergar kept them, would not give them to
      Herward,
His brave young son, though the boy had proved
His loyalty. These are yours: may they serve you well!"
  And after the gleaming armor four horses
Were led in, four bays, swift and all
2165 Alike. Beowulf had brought his king
Horses and treasure—as a man must,
Not weaving nets of malice for his comrades,
Preparing their death in the dark, with secret,
Cunning tricks. Higlac trusted
2170 His nephew, leaned on his strength, in war,
Each of them intent on the other's joy.
And Beowulf gave Welthow's gift, her wonderful
Necklace, to Higd, Higlac's queen,
And gave her, also, three supple, graceful,
2175 Saddle-bright horses; she received his presents,
Then wore that wonderful jewel on her breast.
  So Edgetho's son proved himself,
Did as a famous soldier must do
If glory is what he seeks: not killing his comrades
2180 In drunken rages, his heart not savage,
But guarding God's gracious gift, his strength,
Using it only in war, and then using it
Bravely. And yet as a boy he was scorned;
The Geats considered him worthless. When he sat
2185 In their mead-hall, and their lord was making men
      rich,
He held no claim on the king's good will.
They were sure he was lazy, noble but slow.
The world spun round, he was a warrior more famous
Than any, and all the insults were wiped out.

2190　　　Then Higlac, protector of his people, brought in
　　　　　His father's—Beowulf's grandfather's—great sword,
　　　　　Worked in gold; none of the Geats
　　　　　Could boast of a better weapon. He laid it
　　　　　In Beowulf's lap, then gave him seven
2195　　　Thousand hides of land, houses
　　　　　And ground and all. Geatland was home
　　　　　For both king and prince; their fathers had left them
　　　　　Buildings and fields—but Higlac's inheritance
　　　　　Stretched further, it was he who was king, and was
　　　　　　　followed.

2200　　　Afterwards, in the time when Higlac was dead
　　　　　And Herdred, his son, who'd ruled the Geats
　　　　　After his father, had followed him into darkness—
　　　　　Killed in battle with the Swedes, who smashed
　　　　　His shield, cut through the soldiers surrounding
2205　　　Their king—then, when Higd's one son
　　　　　Was gone, Beowulf ruled in Geatland,
　　　　　Took the throne he'd refused, once,
　　　　　And held it long and well. He was old
　　　　　With years and wisdom, fifty winters
2210　　　A king, when a dragon awoke from its darkness
　　　　　And dreams and brought terror to his people. The
　　　　　　beast
　　　　　Had slept in a huge stone tower, with a hidden
　　　　　Path beneath; a man stumbled on
　　　　　The entrance, went in, discovered the ancient
2215　　　Treasure, the pagan jewels and gold
　　　　　The dragon had been guarding, and dazzled and
　　　　　　greedy
　　　　　Stole a gem-studded cup, and fled.
　　　　　But now the dragon hid nothing, neither
　　　　　The theft nor itself; it swept through the darkness,
2220　　　And all Geatland knew its anger.

32

But the thief had not come to steal; he stole,
And roused the dragon, not from desire
But need. He was someone's slave, had been beaten
By his masters, had run from all men's sight,
2225 But with no place to hide; then he found the hidden
Path, and used it. And once inside,
Seeing the sleeping beast, staring as it
Yawned and stretched, not wanting to wake it,
Terror-struck, he turned and ran for his life,
2230 Taking the jeweled cup.
                That tower
Was heaped high with hidden treasure, stored there
Years before by the last survivor
Of a noble race, ancient riches
2235 Left in the darkness as the end of a dynasty
Came. Death had taken them, one
By one, and the warrior who watched over all
That remained mourned their fate, expecting,
Soon, the same for himself, knowing
2240 The gold and jewels he had guarded so long
Could not bring him pleasure much longer. He
       brought
The precious cups, the armor and the ancient
Swords, to a stone tower built
Near the sea, below a cliff, a sealed
2245 Fortress with no windows, no doors, waves
In front of it, rocks behind. Then he spoke:
    "Take these treasures, earth, now that no one
Living can enjoy them. They were yours, in the
       beginning;
Allow them to return. War and terror
2250 Have swept away my people, shut
Their eyes to delight and to living, closed
The door to all gladness. No one is left
To lift these swords, polish these jeweled
Cups: no one leads, no one follows. These hammered
2255 Helmets, worked with gold, will tarnish
And crack; the hands that should clean and polish
       them
Are still forever. And these mail shirts, worn

In battle, once, while swords crashed
And blades bit into shields and men,
2260   Will rust away like the warriors who owned them.
None of these treasures will travel to distant
Lands, following their lords. The harp's
Bright song, the hawk crossing through the hall
On its swift wings, the stallion tramping
2265   In the courtyard—all gone, creatures of every
Kind, and their masters, hurled to the grave!"
    And so he spoke, sadly, of those
Long dead, and lived from day to day,
Joyless, until, at last, death touched
2270   His heart and took him too. And a stalker
In the night, a flaming dragon, found
The treasure unguarded; he whom men fear
Came flying through the darkness, wrapped in fire,
Seeking caves and stone-split ruins
2275   But finding gold. Then it stayed, buried
Itself with heathen silver and jewels
It could neither use nor ever abandon.
    So mankind's enemy, the mighty beast,
Slept in those stone walls for hundreds
2280   Of years; a runaway slave roused it,
Stole a jeweled cup and bought
His master's forgiveness, begged for mercy
And was pardoned when his delighted lord took the
       present
He bore, turned it in his hands and stared
2285   At the ancient carvings. The cup brought peace
To a slave, pleased his master, but stirred
A dragon's anger. It turned, hunting
The thief's tracks, and found them, saw
Where its visitor had come and gone. He'd survived,
2290   Had come close enough to touch its scaly
Head and yet lived, as it lifted its cavernous
Jaws, through the grace of almighty God
And a pair of quiet, quick-moving feet.
The dragon followed his steps, anxious
2295   To find the man who had robbed it of silver
And sleep; it circled around and around
The tower, determined to catch him, but could not,
He had run too fast, the wilderness was empty.

The beast went back to its treasure, planning
2300 A bloody revenge, and found what was missing,
Saw what thieving hands had stolen.
Then it crouched on the stones, counting off
The hours till the Almighty's candle went out,
And evening came, and wild with anger
2305 It could fly burning across the land, killing
And destroying with its breath. Then the sun was
    gone,
And its heart was glad: glowing with rage
It left the tower, impatient to repay
Its enemies. The people suffered, everyone
2310 Lived in terror, but when Beowulf had learned
Of their trouble his fate was worse, and came quickly.

33

Vomiting fire and smoke, the dragon
Burned down their homes. They watched in horror
As the flames rose up: the angry monster
2315 Meant to leave nothing alive. And the signs
Of its anger flickered and glowed in the darkness,
Visible for miles, tokens of its hate
And its cruelty, spread like a warning to the Geats
Who had broken its rest. Then it hurried back
2320 To its tower, to its hidden treasure, before dawn
Could come. It had wrapped its flames around
The Geats; now it trusted in stone
Walls, and its strength, to protect it. But they would
    not.
Then they came to Beowulf, their king, and
    announced
2325 That his hall, his throne, the best of buildings,
Had melted away in the dragon's burning
Breath. Their words brought misery, Beowulf's
Sorrow beat at his heart: he accused
Himself of breaking God's law, of bringing

2330 The Almighty's anger down on his people.
Reproach pounded in his breast, gloomy
And dark, and the world seemed a different place.
But the hall was gone, the dragon's molten
Breath had licked across it, burned it

2335 To ashes, near the shore it had guarded. The Geats
Deserved revenge; Beowulf, their leader
And lord, began to plan it, ordered
A battle-shield shaped of iron, knowing that
Wood would be useless, that no linden shield

2340 Could help him, protect him, in the flaming heat
Of the beast's breath. That noble prince
would end his days on earth, soon,
Would leave this brief life, but would take the dragon
With him, tear it from the heaped-up treasure

2345 It had guarded so long. And he'd go to it alone,
Scorning to lead soldiers against such
An enemy: he saw nothing to fear, thought nothing
Of the beast's claws, or wings, or flaming
Jaws—he had fought, before, against worse

2350 Odds, had survived, been victorious, in harsher
Battles, beginning in Herot, Hrothgar's
Unlucky hall. He'd killed Grendel
And his mother, swept that murdering tribe
Away. And he'd fought in Higlac's war

2355 With the Frisians, fought at his lord's side
Till a sword reached out and drank Higlac's
Blood, till a blade swung in the rush
Of battle killed the Geats' great king.
Then Beowulf escaped, broke through Frisian

2360 Shields and swam to freedom, saving
Thirty sets of armor from the scavenging
Franks, river people who robbed
The dead as they floated by. Beowulf
Offered them only his sword, ended

2365 So many jackal lives that the few
Who were able skulked silently home, glad
To leave him. So Beowulf swam sadly back
To Geatland, almost the only survivor
Of a foolish war. Higlac's widow

2370 Brought him the crown, offered him the kingdom,
Not trusting Herdred, her son and Higlac's,

To beat off foreign invaders. But Beowulf
Refused to rule when his lord's own son
Was alive, and the leaderless Geats could choose
2375   A rightful king. He gave Herdred
All his support, offering an open
Heart where Higlac's young son could see
Wisdom he still lacked himself: warmth
And good will were what Beowulf brought his new
      king.
2380   But Swedish exiles came, seeking
Protection; they were rebels against Onela,
Healfdane's son-in-law and the best ring-giver
His people had ever known. And Onela
Came too, a mighty king, marched
2385   On Geatland with a huge army; Herdred
Had given his word and now he gave
His life, shielding the Swedish strangers.
Onela wanted nothing more:
When Herdred had fallen that famous warrior
2390   Went back to Sweden, let Beowulf rule!

34

      But Beowulf remembered how his king had been
      killed.
As soon as he could he lent the last
Of the Swedish rebels soldiers and gold,
Helped him to a bitter battle across
2395   The wide sea, where victory, and revenge, and the
      Swedish
Throne were won, and Onela was slain.
      So Edgetho's son survived, no matter
What dangers he met, what battles he fought,
Brave and forever triumphant, till the day
2400   Fate sent him to the dragon and sent him death.
A dozen warriors walked with their angry
King, when he was brought to the beast; Beowulf

Knew, by then, what had woken the monster,
And enraged it. The cup had come to him, traveled
2405   From dragon to slave, to master, to king,
And the slave was their guide, had begun the Geats'
Affliction, and now, afraid of both beast
And men, was forced to lead them to the monster's
Hidden home. He showed them the huge
2410   Stones, set deep in the ground, with the sea
Beating on the rocks close by. Beowulf
Stared, listening to stories of the gold
And riches heaped inside. Hidden,
But wakeful, now, the dragon waited,
2415   Ready to greet him. Gold and hammered
Armor have been buried in pleasanter places!
    The battle-brave king rested on the shore,
While his soldiers wished him well, urged him
On. But Beowulf's heart was heavy:
2420   His soul sensed how close fate
Had come, felt something, not fear but knowledge
Of old age. His armor was strong, but his arm
Hung like his heart. Body and soul
Might part, here; his blood might be spilled,
2425   His spirit torn from his flesh. Then he spoke.
    "My early days were full of war,
And I survived it all; I can remember everything.
I was seven years old when Hrethel opened
His home and his heart for me, when my king and
        lord
2430   Took me from my father and kept me, taught me,
Gave me gold and pleasure, glad that I sat
At his knee. And he never loved me less
Than any of his sons—Herbald, the oldest
Of all, or Hathcyn, or Higlac, my lord.
2435   Herbald died a horrible death,
Killed while hunting: Hathcyn, his brother,
Stretched his horn-tipped bow, sent
An arrow flying, but missed his mark
And hit Herbald instead, found him
2440   With a bloody point and pierced him through.
The crime was great, the guilt was plain,
But nothing could be done, no vengeance, no death
To repay that death, no punishment, nothing.

"So with the graybeard whose son sins
2445 Against the king, and is hanged: he stands
Watching his child swing on the gallows,
Lamenting, helpless, while his flesh and blood
Hangs for the raven to pluck. He can raise
His voice in sorrow, but revenge is impossible.
2450 And every morning he remembers how his son
Died, and despairs; no son to come
Matters, no future heir, to a father
Forced to live through such misery. The place
Where his son once dwelled, before death compelled
  him
2455 To journey away, is a windy wasteland,
Empty, cheerless; the childless father
Shudders, seeing it. So riders and ridden
Sleep in the ground; pleasure is gone,
The harp is silent, and hope is forgotten.

35

2460   "And then, crying his sorrow, he crawls
To his bed: the world, and his home, hurt him
With their emptiness. And so it seemed to Hrethel,
When Herbald was dead, and his heart swelled
With grief. The murderer lived; he felt
2465 No love for him, now, but nothing could help,
Word nor hand nor sharp-honed blade,
War nor hate, battle or blood
Or law. The pain could find no relief,
He could only live with it, or leave grief and life
2470 Together. When he'd gone to his grave Hathcyn
And Higlac, his sons, inherited everything.
    "And then there was war between Geats and
      Swedes,
Bitter battles carried across
The broad sea, when the mighty Hrethel slept
2475 And Ongentho's sons thought Sweden could safely

Attack, saw no use to pretending friendship
But raided and burned, and near old Rennsburg
Slaughtered Geats with their thieving swords.
My people repaid them, death for death,
2480   Battle for battle, though one of the brothers
Bought that revenge with his life—Hathcyn,
King of the Geats, killed by a Swedish
Sword. But when dawn came the slayer
Was slain, and Higlac's soldiers avenged
2485   Everything with the edge of their blades. Efor
Caught the Swedish king, cracked
His helmet, split his skull, dropped him,
Pale and bleeding, to the ground, then put him
To death with a swift stroke, shouting
2490   His joy.
            "The gifts that Higlac gave me,
And the land, I earned with my sword, as fate
Allowed: he never needed Danes
Or Goths or Swedes, soldiers and allies
2495   Bought with gold, bribed to his side.
My sword was better, and always his.
In every battle my place was in front,
Alone, and so it shall be forever,
As long as this sword lasts, serves me
2500   In the future as it has served me before. So
I killed Dagref, the Frank, who brought death
To Higlac, and who looted his corpse: Higd's
Necklace, Welthow's treasure, never
Came to Dagref's king. The thief
2505   Fell in battle, but not on my blade.
He was brave and strong, but I swept him in my arms,
Ground him against me till his bones broke,
Till his blood burst out. And now I shall fight
For this treasure, fight with both hand and sword."
2510   And Beowulf uttered his final boast:
     "I've never known fear; as a youth I fought
In endless battles. I am old, now,
But I will fight again, seek fame still,
If the dragon hiding in his tower dares
2515   To face me."
            Then he said farewell to his followers,
Each in his turn, for the last time:

"I'd use no sword, no weapon, if this beast
Could be killed without it, crushed to death
2520 Like Grendel, gripped in my hands and torn
Limb from limb. But his breath will be burning
Hot, poison will pour from his tongue.
I feel no shame, with shield and sword
And armor, against this monster: when he comes
      to me
2525 I mean to stand, not run from his shooting
Flames, stand till fate decides
Which of us wins. My heart is firm,
My hands calm: I need no hot
Words. Wait for me close by, my friends.
2530 We shall see, soon, who will survive
This bloody battle, stand when the fighting
Is done. No one else could do
What I mean to, here, no man but me
Could hope to defeat this monster. No one
2535 Could try. And this dragon's treasure, his gold
And everything hidden in that tower, will be mine
Or war will sweep me to a bitter death!"
    Then Beowulf rose, still brave, still strong,
And with his shield at his side, and a mail shirt on his
      breast,
2540 Strode calmly, confidently, toward the tower, under
The rocky cliffs: no coward could have walked there!
And then he who'd endured dozens of desperate
Battles, who'd stood boldly while swords and shields
Clashed, the best of kings, saw
2545 Huge stone arches and felt the heat
Of the dragon's breath, flooding down
Through the hidden entrance, too hot for anyone
To stand, a streaming current of fire
And smoke that blocked all passage. And the Geats'
2550 Lord and leader, angry, lowered
His sword and roared out a battle cry,
A call so loud and clear that it reached through
The hoary rock, hung in the dragon's
Ear. The beast rose, angry,
2555 Knowing a man had come—and then nothing
But war could have followed. Its breath came first.
A steaming cloud pouring from the stone,

Then the earth itself shook. Beowulf
Swung his shield into place, held it
2560 In front of him, facing the entrance. The dragon
Coiled and uncoiled, its heart urging it
Into battle. Beowulf's ancient sword
Was waiting, unsheathed, his sharp and gleaming
Blade. The beast came closer; both of them
2565 Were ready, each set on slaughter. The Geats'
Great prince stood firm, unmoving, prepared
Behind his high shield, waiting in his shining
Armor. The monster came quickly toward him,
Pouring out fire and smoke, hurrying
2570 To its fate. Flames beat at the iron
Shield, and for a time it held, protected
Beowulf as he'd planned; then it began to melt,
And for the first time in his life that famous prince
Fought with fate against him, with glory
2575 Denied him. He knew it, but he raised his sword
And struck at the dragon's scaly hide.
The ancient blade broke, bit into
The monster's skin, drew blood, but cracked
And failed him before it went deep enough, helped
        him
2580 Less than he needed. The dragon leaped
With pain, thrashed and beat at him, spouting
Murderous flames, spreading them everywhere.
And the Geats' ring-giver did not boast of glorious
Victories in other wars: his weapon
2585 Had failed him, deserted him, now when he needed it
Most, that excellent sword. Edgetho's
Famous son stared at death,
Unwilling to leave this world, to exchange it
For a dwelling in some distant place—a journey
2590 Into darkness that all men must make, as death
Ends their few brief hours on earth.
        Quickly, the dragon came at him, encouraged
As Beowulf fell back; its breath flared,
And he suffered, wrapped around in swirling
2595 Flames—a king, before, but now
A beaten warrior. None of his comrades
Came to him, helped him, his brave and noble
Followers; they ran for their lives, fled

Deep in a wood. And only one of them
2600 Remained, stood there, miserable, remembering,
As a good man must, what kinship should mean.

36

His name was Wiglaf, he was Wexstan's son
And a good soldier; his family had been Swedish,
Once. Watching Beowulf, he could see
2605 How his king was suffering, burning. Remembering
Everything his lord and cousin had given him,
Armor and gold and the great estates
Wexstan's family enjoyed, Wiglaf's
Mind was made up; he raised his yellow
2610 Shield and drew his sword—an ancient
Weapon that had once belonged to Onela's
Nephew, and that Wexstan had won, killing
The prince when he fled from Sweden, sought safety
With Herdred, and found death. And Wiglaf's father
2615 Had carried the dead man's armor, and his sword,
To Onela, and the king had said nothing, only
Given him armor and sword and all,
Everything his rebel nephew had owned
And lost when he left this life. And Wexstan
2620 Had kept those shining gifts, held them
For years, waiting for his son to use them,
Wear them as honorably and well as once
His father had done; then Wexstan died
And Wiglaf was his heir, inherited treasures
2625 And weapons and land. He'd never worn
That armor, fought with that sword, until Beowulf
Called him to his side, led him into war.
But his soul did not melt, his sword was strong;
The dragon discovered his courage, and his weapon,
2630 When the rush of battle brought them together.
And Wiglaf, his heart heavy, uttered
The kind of words his comrades deserved:

"I remember how we sat in the mead-hall, drinking
And boasting of how brave we'd be when Beowulf
2635 Needed us, he who gave us these swords
And armor: all of us swore to repay him,
When the time came, kindness for kindness
—With our lives, if he needed them. He allowed us to
      join him,
Chose us from all his great army, thinking
2640 Our boasting words had some weight, believing
Our promises, trusting our swords. He took us
For soldiers, for men. He meant to kill
This monster himself, our mighty king,
Fight this battle alone and unaided,
2645 As in the days when his strength and daring dazzled
Men's eyes. But those days are over and gone
And now our lord must lean on younger
Arms. And we must go to him, while angry
Flames burn at his flesh, help
2650 Our glorious king! By almighty God,
I'd rather burn myself than see
Flames swirling around my lord.
And who are we to carry home
Our shields before we've slain his enemy
2655 And ours, to run back to our homes with Beowulf
So hard-pressed here? I swear that nothing
He ever did deserved an end
Like this, dying miserably and alone,
Butchered by this savage beast: we swore
2660 That these swords and armor were each for us all!"
      Then he ran to his king, crying encouragement
As he dove through the dragon's deadly fumes:
      "Belovèd Beowulf, remember how you boasted,
Once, that nothing in the world would ever
2665 Destroy your fame: fight to keep it,
Now, be strong and brave, my noble
King, protecting life and fame
Together. My sword will fight at your side!"
      The dragon heard him, the man-hating monster,
2670 And was angry; shining with surging flames
It came for him, anxious to return his visit.
Waves of fire swept at his shield
And the edge began to burn. His mail shirt

Could not help him, but before his hands dropped
2675   The blazing wood Wiglaf jumped
Behind Beowulf's shield; his own was burned
To ashes. Then the famous old hero, remembering
Days of glory, lifted what was left
Of Nagling, his ancient sword, and swung it
2680   With all his strength, smashed the gray
Blade into the beast's head. But then Nagling
Broke to pieces, as iron always
Had in Beowulf's hands. His arms
Were too strong, the hardest blade could not help
      him,
2685   The most wonderfully worked. He carried them to war
But fate had decreed that the Geats' great king
Would be no better for any weapon.
    Then the monster charged again, vomiting
Fire, wild with pain, rushed out
2690   Fierce and dreadful, its fear forgotten.
Watching for its chance it drove its tusks
Into Beowulf's neck; he staggered, the blood
Came flooding forth, fell like rain.

37

    And then when Beowulf needed him most
2695   Wiglaf showed his courage, his strength
And skill, and the boldness he was born with.
    Ignoring
The dragon's head, he helped his lord
By striking lower down. The sword
Sank in; his hand was burned, but the shining
2700   Blade had done its work, the dragon's
Belching flames began to flicker
And die away. And Beowulf drew
His battle-sharp dagger: the blood-stained old king
Still knew what he was doing. Quickly, he cut
2705   The beast in half, slit it apart.

It fell, their courage had killed it, two noble
Cousins had joined in the dragon's death.
Yet what they did all men must do
When the time comes! But the triumph was the last
2710 Beowulf would ever earn, the end
Of greatness and life together. The wound
In his neck began to swell and grow;
He could feel something stirring, burning
In his veins, a stinging venom, and knew
2715 The beast's fangs had left it. He fumbled
Along the wall, found a slab
Of stone, and dropped down; above him he saw
Huge stone arches and heavy posts,
Holding up the roof of that giant hall.
2720 Then Wiglaf's gentle hands bathed
The blood-stained prince, his glorious lord,
Weary of war, and loosened his helmet.
      Beowulf spoke, in spite of the swollen,
Livid wound, knowing he'd unwound
2725 His string of days on earth, seen
As much as God would grant him; all worldly
Pleasure was gone, as life would go,
Soon:
            "I'd leave my armor to my son,
2730 Now, if God had given me an heir,
A child born of my body, his life
Created from mine. I've worn this crown
For fifty winters: no neighboring people
Have tried to threaten the Geats, sent soldiers
2735 Against us or talked of terror. My days
Have gone by as fate willed, waiting
For its word to be spoken, ruling as well
As I knew how, swearing no unholy oaths,
Seeking no lying wars. I can leave
2740 This life happy; I can die, here,
Knowing the Lord of all life has never
Watched me wash my sword in blood
Born of my own family. Belovèd
Wiglaf, go, quickly, find
2745 The dragon's treasure: we've taken its life,
But its gold is ours, too. Hurry,
Bring me ancient silver, precious

Jewels, shining armor and gems,
Before I die. Death will be softer,
2750   Leaving life and this people I've ruled
So long, if I look at this last of all prizes."

38

Then Wexstan's son went in, as quickly
As he could, did as the dying Beowulf
Asked, entered the inner darkness
2755   Of the tower, went with his mail shirt and his sword.
Flushed with victory he groped his way,
A brave young warrior, and suddenly saw
Piles of gleaming gold, precious
Gems, scattered on the floor, cups
2760   And bracelets, rusty old helmets, beautifully
Made but rotting with no hands to rub
And polish them. They lay where the dragon left
    them;
It had flown in the darkness, once, before fighting
Its final battle. (So gold can easily
2765   Triumph, defeat the strongest of men,
No matter how deep it is hidden!) And he saw,
Hanging high above, a golden
Banner, woven by the best of weavers
And beautiful. And over everything he saw
2770   A strange light, shining everywhere,
On walls and floor and treasure. Nothing
Moved, no other monsters appeared;
He took what he wanted, all the treasures
That pleased his eye, heavy plates
2775   And golden cups and the glorious banner,
Loaded his arms with all they could hold.
Beowulf's dagger, his iron blade,
Had finished the fire-spitting terror
That once protected tower and treasures
2780   Alike; the gray-bearded lord of the Geats

Had ended those flying, burning raids
Forever.
           Then Wiglaf went back, anxious
To return while Beowulf was alive, to bring him
2785 Treasure they'd won together. He ran,
hoping his wounded king, weak
And dying, had not left the world too soon.
Then he brought their treasure to Beowulf, and found
His famous king bloody, gasping
2790 For breath. But Wiglaf sprinkled water
Over his lord, until the words
Deep in his breast broke through and were heard.
Beholding the treasure he spoke, haltingly:
           "For this, this gold, these jewels, I thank
2795 Our Father in Heaven, Ruler of the Earth—
For all of this, that His grace has given me,
Allowed me to bring to my people while breath
Still came to my lips. I sold my life
For this treasure, and I sold it well. Take
2800 What I leave, Wiglaf, lead my people,
Help them; my time is gone. Have
The brave Geats build me a tomb,
When the funeral flames have burned me, and build it
Here, at the water's edge, high
2805 On this spit of land, so sailors can see
This tower, and remember my name, and call it
Beowulf's tower, and boats in the darkness
And mist, crossing the sea, will know it."
           Then that brave king gave the golden
2810 Necklace from around his throat to Wiglaf,
Gave him his gold-covered helmet, and his rings,
And his mail shirt, and ordered him to use them well:
           "You're the last of all our far-flung family.
Fate has swept our race away,
2815 Taken warriors in their strength and led them
To the death that was waiting. And now I follow
           them."
           The old man's mouth was silent, spoke
No more, had said as much as it could;
He would sleep in the fire, soon. His soul
2820 Left his flesh, flew to glory.

39

And then Wiglaf was left, a young warrior
Sadly watching his belovèd king,
Seeing him stretched on the ground, left guarding
A torn and bloody corpse. But Beowulf's
2825 Killer was dead, too, the coiled
Dragon, cut in half, cold
And motionless: men, and their swords, had swept it
From the earth, left it lying in front of
Its tower, won its treasure when it fell
2830 Crashing to the ground, cut it apart
With their hammered blades, driven them deep in
Its belly. It would never fly through the night,
Glowing in the dark sky, glorying
In its riches, burning and raiding: two warriors
2835 Had shown it their strength, slain it with their swords.
Not many men, no matter how strong,
No matter how daring, how bold, had done
As well, rushing at its venomous fangs,
Or even quietly entering its tower,
2840 Intending to steal but finding the treasure's
Guardian awake, watching and ready
To greet them. Beowulf had gotten its gold,
Bought it with blood; dragon and king
Had ended each other's days on earth.
2845 And when the battle was over Beowulf's followers
Came out of the wood, cowards and traitors,
Knowing the dragon was dead. Afraid,
While it spit its fires, to fight in their lord's
Defense, to throw their javelins and spears,
2850 They came like shamefaced jackals, their shields
In their hands, to the place where the prince lay dead,
And waited for Wiglaf to speak. He was sitting
Near Beowulf's body, wearily sprinkling
Water in the dead man's face, trying
2855 To stir him. He could not. No one could have kept
Life in their lord's body, or turned
Aside the Lord's will: world
And men and all move as He orders,
And always have, and always will.
2860 Then Wiglaf turned and angrily told them

What men without courage must hear.
Wexstan's brave son stared at the traitors,
His heart sorrowful, and said what he had to:
   "I say what anyone who speaks the truth

2865   Must say. Your lord gave you gifts,
Swords and the armor you stand in now;
You sat on the mead-hall benches, prince
And followers, and he gave you, with open hands,
Helmets and mail shirts, hunted across

2870   The world for the best of weapons. War
Came and you ran like cowards, dropped
Your swords as soon as the danger was real.
Should Beowulf have boasted of your help, rejoiced
In your loyal strength? With God's good grace

2875   He helped himself, swung his sword
Alone, won his own revenge.
The help I gave him was nothing, but all
I was able to give; I went to him, knowing
That nothing but Beowulf's strength could save us,

2880   And my sword was lucky, found some vital
Place and bled the burning flames
Away. Too few of his warriors remembered
To come, when our lord faced death, alone.
And now the giving of swords, of golden

2885   Rings and rich estates, is over,
Ended for you and everyone who shares
Your blood: when the brave Geats hear
How you bolted and ran none of your race
Will have anything left but their lives. And death

2890   Would be better for them all, and for you, than the
        kind
Of life you can lead, branded with disgrace!"

40

Then Wiglaf ordered a messenger to ride
Across the cliff, to the Geats who'd waited
The morning away, sadly wondering
2895　If their belovèd king would return, or be killed,
A troop of soldiers sitting in silence
And hoping for the best. Whipping his horse
The herald came to them; they crowded around,
And he told them everything, present and past:
2900　　"Our lord is dead, leader of this people.
The dragon killed him, but the beast is dead,
Too, cut in half by a dagger;
Beowulf's enemy sleeps in its blood.
No sword could pierce its skin, wound
2905　That monster. Wiglaf is sitting in mourning,
Close to Beowulf's body, Wexstan's
Weary son, silent and sad,
Keeping watch for our king, there
Where Beowulf and the beast that killed him lie dead.
2910　　"And this people can expect fighting, once
The Franks, and the Frisians, have heard that our king
Lies dead. The news will spread quickly.
Higlac began our bitter quarrel
With the Franks, raiding along their river
2915　Rhine with ships and soldiers, until
They attacked him with a huge army, and Higlac
Was killed, the king and many of our men,
Mailed warriors defeated in war,
Beaten by numbers. He brought no treasure
2920　To the mead-hall, after that battle. And ever
After we knew no friendship with the Franks.
　　"Nor can we expect peace from the Swedes.
Everyone knows how their old king,
Ongentho, killed Hathcyn, caught him
2925　Near a wood when our young lord went
To war too soon, dared too much.
The wise old Swede, always terrible
In war, allowed the Geats to land
And begin to loot, then broke them with a lightning
2930　Attack, taking back treasure and his kidnaped
Queen, and taking our king's life.

And then he followed his beaten enemies,
Drove them in front of Swedish swords
Until darkness dropped, and weary, lordless,
2935 They could hide in the wood. But he waited,
    Ongentho
With his mass of soldiers, circled around
The Geats who'd survived, who'd escaped him, calling
Threats and boasts at that wretched band
The whole night through. In the morning he'd hang
2940 A few, he promised, to amuse the birds,
Then slaughter the rest. But the sun rose
To the sound of Higlac's horns and trumpets,
Light and that battle cry coming together
And turning sadhearted Geats into soldiers.
2945 Higlac had followed his people, and found them.

41

"Then blood was everywhere, two bands of Geats
Falling on the Swedes, men fighting
On all sides, butchering each other.
Sadly, Ongentho ordered his soldiers
2950 Back, to the high ground where he'd built
A fortress; he'd heard of Higlac, knew
His boldness and strength. Out in the open
He could never resist such a soldier, defend
Hard-won treasure, Swedish wives
2955 And children, against the Geats' new king.
Brave but wise, he fled, sought safety
Behind earthen walls. Eagerly, the Geats
Followed, sweeping across the field,
Smashing through the walls, waving Higlac's
2960 Banners as they came. Then the gray-haired old king
Was brought to bay, bright sword-blades
Forcing the lord of the Swedes to take
Judgment at Efor's hands. Efor's
Brother, Wulf, raised his weapon

2965   First, swung it angrily at the fierce
         Old king, cracked his helmet; blood
         Seeped through his hair. But the brave old Swede
         Felt no fear: he quickly returned
         A better blow than he'd gotten, faced
2970   Toward Wulf and struck him savagely. And Efor's
         Bold brother was staggered, half raised his sword
         But only dropped it to the ground. Ongentho's
         Blade had cut through his helmet, his head
         Spouted blood, and slowly he fell.
2975   The wound was deep, but death was not due
         So soon; fate let him recover, live
         On. But Efor, his brave brother,
         Seeing Wulf fall, came forward with his broadbladed
         Sword, hammered by giants, and swung it
2980   So hard that Ongentho's shield shattered
         And he sank to the earth, his life ended.
         Then, with the battlefield theirs, the Geats
         Rushed to Wulf's side, raised him up
         and bound his wound. Wulf's brother
2985   Stripped the old Swede, took
         His iron mail shirt, his hilted sword
         And his helmet, and all his ancient war-gear,
         And brought them to Higlac, his new lord.
         The king welcomed him, warmly thanked him
2990   For his gifts and promised, there where everyone
         Could hear, that as soon as he sat in his mead-hall
         Again Efor and Wulf would have treasure
         Heaped in their battle-hard hands; he'd repay them
         Their bravery with wealth, give them gold
2995   And lands and silver rings, rich rewards for the
             glorious
         Deeds they'd done with their swords. The Geats
             agreed. And to prove
         Efor's grace in his eyes, Higlac
         Swore he'd give him his only daughter.
           "These are the quarrels, the hatreds, the feuds,
3000   That will bring us battles, force us into war
         With the Swedes, as soon as they've learned how our
             lord
         Is dead, know that the Geats are leaderless,
         Have lost the best of kings, Beowulf—

He who held our enemies away,
3005 Kept land and treasure intact, who saved
Hrothgar and the Danes—he who lived
All his long life bravely. Then let us
Go to him, hurry to our glorious lord,
Behold him lifeless, and quickly carry him
3010 To the flames. The fire must melt more
Than his bones, more than his share of treasure:
Give it all of this golden pile,
This terrible, uncounted heap of cups
And rings, bought with his blood. Burn it
3015 To ashes, to nothingness. No one living
Should enjoy these jewels; no beautiful women
Wear them, gleaming and golden, from their necks,
But walk, instead, sad and alone
In a hundred foreign lands, their laughter
3020 Gone forever, as Beowulf's has gone,
His pleasure and his joy. Spears shall be lifted,
Many cold mornings, lifted and thrown,
And warriors shall waken to no harp's bright call
But the croak of the dark-black raven, ready
3025 To welcome the dead, anxious to tell
The eagle how he stuffed his craw with corpses,
Filled his belly even faster than the wolves."
      And so the messenger spoke, a brave
Man on an ugly errand, telling
3030 Only the truth. Then the warriors rose,
Walked slowly down from the cliff, stared
At those wonderful sights, stood weeping as they saw
Beowulf dead on the sand, their bold
Ring-giver resting in his last bed;
3035 He'd reached the end of his days, their mighty
War-king, the great lord of the Geats,
Gone to a glorious death. But they saw
The dragon first, stretched in front
Of its tower, a strange, scaly beast
3040 Gleaming a dozen colors dulled and
Scorched in its own heat. From end
To end fifty feet, it had flown
In the silent darkness, a swift traveler
Tasting the air, then gliding down
3045 To its den. Death held it in his hands;

It would guard no caves, no towers, keep
No treasures like the cups, the precious plates
Spread where it lay, silver and brass
Encrusted and rotting, eaten away
3050   As though buried in the earth for a thousand winters.
And all this ancient hoard, huge
And golden, was wound around with a spell:
No man could enter the tower, open
Hidden doors, unless the Lord
3055   Of Victories, He who watches over men,
Almighty God Himself, was moved
To let him enter, and him alone.

42

Hiding that treasure deep in its tower,
As the dragon had done, broke God's law
3060   And brought it no good. Guarding its stolen
Wealth it killed Wiglaf's king,
But was punished with death. Who knows when
        princes
And their soldiers, the bravest and strongest of men,
Are destined to die, their time ended,
3065   Their homes, their halls empty and still?
So Beowulf sought out the dragon, dared it
Into battle, but could never know what God
Had decreed, or that death would come to him, or
        why.
So the spell was solemnly laid, by men
3070   Long dead; it was meant to last till the day
Of judgment. Whoever stole their jewels,
Their gold, would be cursed with the flames of hell,
Heaped high with sin and guilt, if greed
Was what brought him: God alone could break
3075   Their magic, open His grace to man.
    Then Wiglaf spoke, Wexstan's son:
    "How often an entire country suffers

On one man's account! That time has come to us:
We tried to counsel our belovèd king,
3080 Our shield and protection, show him danger,
Urge him to leave the dragon in the dark
Tower it had lain in so long, live there
Till the end of the world. Fate, and his will,
Were too strong. Everyone knows the treasure
3085 His life bought: but Beowulf was worth
More than this gold, and the gift is a harsh one.
I've seen it all, been in the tower
Where the jewels and armor were hidden, allowed
To behold them once war and its terror were done.
3090 I gathered them up, gold and silver,
Filled my arms as full as I could
And quickly carried them back to my king.
He lay right here, still alive,
Still sure in mind and tongue. He spoke
3095 Sadly, said I should greet you, asked
That after you'd burned his body you bring
His ashes here, make this the tallest
Of towers and his tomb—as great and lasting
As his fame, when Beowulf himself walked
3100 The earth and no man living could match him.
Come, let us enter the tower, see
The dragon's marvelous treasure one
Last time: I'll lead the way, take you
Close to that heap of curious jewels,
3105 And rings, and gold. Let the pyre be ready
And high: as soon as we've seen the dragon's
Hoard we will carry our belovèd king,
Our leader and lord, where he'll lie forever
In God's keeping."
3110   Then Wiglaf commanded
The wealthiest Geats, brave warriors
And owners of land, leaders of his people,
To bring wood for Beowulf's funeral:
    "Now the fire must feed on his body,
3115 Flames grow heavy and black with him
Who endured arrows falling in iron
Showers, feathered shafts, barbed
And sharp, shot through linden shields,
Storms of eager arrowheads dropping."

3120   And Wextan's wise son took seven
Of the noblest Geats, led them together
Down the tunnel, deep into the dragon's
Tower; the one in front had a torch,
Held it high in his hands. The best
3125   Of Beowulf's followers entered behind
That gleaming flame: seeing gold
And silver rotting on the ground, with no one
To guard it, the Geats were not troubled with scruples
Or fears, but quickly gathered up
3130   Treasure and carried it out of the tower.
And they rolled the dragon down to the cliff
And dropped it over, let the ocean take it,
The tide sweep it away. Then silver
And gold and precious jewels were put
3135   On a wagon, with Beowulf's body, and brought
down the jutting sand, where the pyre waited.

43

A huge heap of wood was ready,
Hung around with helmets, and battle
Shields, and shining mail shirts, all
3140   As Beowulf had asked. The bearers brought
Their belovèd lord, their glorious king,
And weeping laid him high on the wood.
Then the warriors began to kindle that greatest
Of funeral fires; smoke rose
3145   Above the flames, black and thick,
And while the wind blew and the fire
Roared they wept, and Beowulf's body
Crumbled and was gone. The Geats stayed,
Moaning their sorrow, lamenting their lord:
3150   A gnarled old woman, hair wound
Tight and gray on her head, groaned
A song of misery, of infinite sadness
And days of mourning, of fear and sorrow

To come, slaughter and terror and captivity.
3155 And Heaven swallowed the billowing smoke.
  Then the Geats built the tower, as Beowulf
Had asked, strong and tall, so sailors
Could find it from far and wide; working
For ten long days they made his monument,
3160 Sealed his ashes in walls as straight
And high as wise and willing hands
Could raise them. And the riches he and Wiglaf
Had won from the dragon, rings, necklaces,
Ancient, hammered armor—all
3165 The treasures they'd taken were left there, too,
Silver and jewels buried in the sandy
Ground, back in the earth, again
And forever hidden and useless to men.
And then twelve of the bravest Geats
3170 Rode their horses around the tower,
Telling their sorrow, telling stories
Of their dead king and his greatness, his glory,
Praising him for heroic deeds, for a life
As noble as his name. So should all men
3175 Raise up words for their lords, warm
With love, when their shield and protector leaves
His body behind, sends his soul
On high. And so Beowulf's followers
Rode, mourning their belovèd leader,
3180 Crying that no better king had ever
Lived, no prince so mild, no man
So open to his people, so deserving of praise.

Glossary of Names

Persons, peoples, and places are here alphabetically arranged according to the form used in this translation.

BEO: a Danish king, Shild's son, Healfdane's father.

BEOWULF: Possibly mythical son of Edgetho, Higlac's nephew and follower, and later king of the Geats. Following the chronology implicit in the poem, Beowulf was born in A.D. 495, went to Denmark and to Hrothgar's help in 515, accompanied Higlac on his expedition against the Franks and Frisians in 521, became king of the Geats in 533, and died at some indefinite later date. The "fifty years" of his reign are, as Friedrich Klaeber notes, only "a sort of poetic formula."

BONSTAN: father of Brecca.

BRECCA: chief of a tribe known as the Brondings; a contemporary and young companion of Beowulf. His father is Bonstan.

BRONDINGS: a (Scandinavian?) tribe about whom nothing, including their location, seems to be known.

BROSING: possibly a reference to Breisach, on the Rhine near Freiburg; possibly a reference to the Brisings, who made a marvelous necklace for the goddess Freyja (see the Norse Elder Edda).

DAGREF: a Frank warrior, Higlac's killer, who is killed by Beowulf.

ECLAF: Unferth's father.

EDGETHO: Beowulf's father, a notable warrior married to Hrethel's one daughter (Beowulf's mother is never named).

EFOR: a Geat warrior, who kills Ongentho, the Swedish king, and is given Higlac's daughter as a reward.

EMER: son of Offa.

ERMLAF: a Danish nobleman, younger brother of Esher.

ERMRIC: a king of the East Goths, historical but converted into the very model of a medieval tyrant; he is so portrayed in the Old English poems "Deor" and "Widsith."

ESHER: a Danish nobleman, high in the councils of King Hrothgar, and long his close and trusted friend. Esher is killed by Grendel's mother.

FINN: a Frisian king, married to Hnaf's sister.

FITLA: son (and nephew) of Siegmund. His role, in this and other similar stories, is quite dissimilar to that of Siegfried, who is Siegmund's son (and nephew) in the *Nibelungenlied* and in the Wagner operas.

FRANKS: a West German people, resident near the Rhine and the Meuse rivers. A Frankish tribe conquered Gaul, about A.D. 500, and gave its name to modern France.

FREAW: a Danish princess, Hrothgar's daughter. She is given in marriage to Ingeld, a Hathobard prince, in the vain hope of settling the feud between the two peoples.

FRISIANS: a West German people, resident in what is now northwestern Holland.

FRODA: chief of the Hathobards, Ingeld's father.

GARMUND: Offa's father.

GEATS: a people of southern Sweden, the Gøtar, conquered by the Swedish kingdom in about the sixth century A.D. Infinite ink has been spilled about the precise identification of this people, and their homeland; any and all Old English editions of *Beowulf* (or a fine compendium like R. W. Chambers' *Beowulf*) can lead the interested as far as—and probably further than—he cares to go.

GOTHS: I have here substituted the well-known Goths for their virtually unknown cousins, the *Gifthas*. The latter tribe emigrated from lands near the mouth of the Vistula (a river in Poland) about the third century A.D., settled near the lower Danube, and were wiped out as an independent political entity by the Lombards, toward the end of the sixth century A.D.

GRENDEL: a man-eating monster who terrorizes the Danes until killed by Beowulf. Grendel lives, with his equally monstrous mother, at the bottom of a foul lake inhabited by assorted other monsters; he is descended from Cain (the progenitor of all evil spirits), though his precise genealogy is not given. The etymology of his name is conjectural: it is perhaps related to Old Norse *grindill*, "storm," and *grenja*, "to bellow," and to other words meaning "sand," "ground (bottom) of a body of water," and "grinder (destroyer)."

HALGA: a Danish prince, third son of Healfdane, younger brother of King Hrothgar, and father of Hrothulf. Halga predeceased king Hrothgar by some twenty years. The epithet "good" may have been given him for strictly metrical reasons; nothing in the poem explains it.

HAMA: a character in the cycle of stories about Ermric (and Theodoric, not mentioned in *Beowulf*). Precisely what role Hama is supposed to have played, in the poem's oblique reference to him, is not understood.

HARETH: Higd's father, apparently a prosperous man of standing.

HATHCYN: a king of the Geats, Hrethel's second son, who ascends the throne after he accidentally kills his older brother, Herbald, and their father has died of grief. Hathcyn is killed by Ongentho, king of the Swedes, in a war which then sees Ongentho killed by a second band of Geats, led by Higlac.

HATHLAF: a Wulfing warrior, slain by Edgetho; his death causes a feud which is settled, after Edgetho has been exiled, by the intercession (and gold) of Hrothgar.

HATHOBARDS: a seafaring German tribe, sometimes identified with the Lombards (who had not yet migrated down toward Italy), sometimes with the Erulians, but not definitely placed either historically or geographically. They may have lived, at least for a time, on the south Baltic coast.

HEALFDANE: a Danish king, Beo's son, and father of Hergar, Hrothgar, Halga, and Urs. Whether or not the name means Half-Dane is uncertain.

HEMMING: a kinsman of Offa, though in what precise relationship is not known.

HENGEST: a Danish warrior, Hnaf's chief lieutenant and, de facto, his successor.

HERBALD: a prince of the Geats, Hrethel's oldest son. He is killed, in a hunting accident, by his brother, Hathcyn, and his necessarily unavenged death causes his father to die of grief. The parallel with the Balder (Baldr) myth has often been noted.

HERDRED: a king of the Geats, Higlac's son, killed by the powerful Swedish king, Onela.

HERGAR: a Danish king, oldest son of Healfdane, older brother and predecessor of Hrothgar, and father of Herward. His reign was apparently a brief one.

HERMOD: an archetypal but partly historical Danish king, of great military prowess combined with the lowest possible character. Like Wayland, the famous smith, Hermod is mentioned frequently in the poetry of other Germanic languages.

HEROT: the lofty battle hall built by King Hrothgar, to celebrate his victories, house his growing band of followers, and perhaps to perpetuate his fame. As the poet hints, in lines 84–85, a coming war will result in the burning down of Herot.

HERWARD: Hergar's son. He seems to have been by-passed, at his father's death (his uncle Hrothgar taking the throne), either because he was thought too young to rule or because he had been out of favor with his father. See lines 2160–2162, and see under Hrothulf, below.

HIGD: Higlac's wife, Hareth's daughter. Her name means "thoughtful," or "prudent."

HIGLAC: a king of the Geats, Hrethel's son, younger brother of Herbald and Hathcyn. Higlac is both Beowulf's feudal lord and his uncle.

HNAF: a Danish king, killed by Finn; his sister was Finn's wife.

HONDSHEW: a Geat warrior, one of Beowulf's companions on the journey to King Hrothgar's court. Hondshew is the man killed and eaten by Grendel, on the evening when the Geats instead of the Danes lay sleeping in Herot, Hrothgar's hall—the evening when Beowulf, instead of becoming the monster's second victim, gave Grendel his mortal wound.

HRETHEL: a king of the Geats, Higlac's father, Beowulf's grandfather.

HRETHRIC: the older of Hrothgar's two young sons.

HROTHGAR: a Danish king, second son of Healfdane, builder of Herot, and beneficiary of Beowulf's courage. One of the principal characters of the poem, he is depicted as near the end of his life, wise, brave, but troubled, remembering his glorious past, afflicted with first Grendel and then Grendel's monstrous mother, and worried about the fate of his sons, at his nephew Hrothulf's hands, after his imminent death. Hrothgar has befriended Beowulf's father, which more than satisfactorily accounts for the help Beowulf gives him.

HROTHMUND: the younger of Hrothgar's two young sons.

HROTHULF: Halga's son, Hrothgar's nephew. Although Welthow, Hrothgar's queen, invokes the spirit of good will prevailing at the Danish court, and predicts that Hrothulf will guard her two young sons, the Anglo-Saxon listener knew that Hrothulf was later to seize the throne, after Hrothgar's death, and also was to murder Hrethric, Hrothgar's legal heir. Hrothulf, the Anglo-Saxon listener knew further, was subsequently to be killed by Hergar's son, Herward—but none of this is stated in the poem.

HRUNTING: Unferth's ancient sword. Few things show more clearly the importance of weapons (and armor), in Anglo-Saxon culture, than their being assigned names—and, on occasion, other personalized characteristics.

INGELD: a prince of the Hathobards, Froda's son, married to Freaw, the Danish princess.

JUTES: a Frisian people, or a people allied with (and possibly subordinate to?) the Frisians.

NAGLING: the name of Beowulf's sword. (See under Hrunting, above.)

OFFA: a king of the Angles—those of them who did not migrate to Angle-land (England) but remained on the European continent. Offa is the husband and tamer of Thrith. Various historical and mythological narratives are fused in this briefly told tale (see also the Old English poem "Widsith").

ONELA: a Swedish king, younger son of Ongentho, and husband of the Danish king Healfdane's daughter. Onela seized the Swedish throne, after his older brother's death; his brother's sons fled to Herdred, king of the Geats. The Swedish king thereupon invaded Geatland, killed Herdred and the older of his two nephews (the legal heir to the Swedish throne), but then returned home and permitted Beowulf to rule Geatland. However, Beowulf soon supported an invasion of Sweden by the surviving nephew, and the latter took both Onela's life and his throne. The poet regards Onela as something of a model king.

ONGENTHO: a Swedish king, mighty in battle, and obviously respected by the poet. In the fighting which followed Hrethel's death, Ongentho first killed Hathcyn, the Geats' king, and was then himself killed by another group of Geats, led by Higlac. Ongentho is Onela's father.

RENNSBURG: the location of the battle between Swedes and Geats, in which first Hathcyn and then Ongentho are killed.

SHILD: a Danish king, Beo's father, Healfdane's grandfather, and Hrothgar's great-grandfather. Shild is mythological; he has Scandinavian analogues, as Skjǫldr, and scholars have elaborated a variety of possible religious/agricultural meanings for his story.

SIEGMUND: son of Vels, father (and uncle) of Fitla. This is the *Nibelungenlied* (and Wagner's) Siegmund in one of his assorted other incarnations.

SWERTING: Higlac's grandfather.

THRITH: Offa's wife, and a type of haughty, violent young woman very like Katharina, in Shakespeare's *The Taming of the Shrew*. Like Katharina, Thrith is tamed and gentled by a husband stronger even than she; unlike *The Taming of the Shrew*, the poem does not tell us precisely how the miracle was accomplished.

UNFERTH: one of Hrothgar's courtiers, skillful with words, and also a man of considerable reputation as a warrior; his father is Ecglaf. Unferth's sword, lent to Beowulf for the fight with Grendel's mother, is called Hrunting.

VELS: Siegmund's father. The familial name is, in this version of the story, derived from Vǫlsung, in the Norse saga.

WAYLAND: a smith celebrated in many surviving Germanic poems; to ascribe a sword or a mail shirt to his gifted hammer was to evoke an automatic association of wonderful workmanship and, in most cases, also of wonderful men and deeds. Wayland is mentioned at some length in "Deor," perhaps the oldest surviving Old English poem (see Raffel, *Poems from the Old English* [1960], pp. 39–40).

WELTHOW: Hrothgar's queen, and the mother of his young sons, Hrethric and Hrothmund. Most of her speeches are full of tragic implications, well-known to the Anglo-Saxon audience. (See under Hrothulf, above.)

WEXSTAN: Wiglaf's father, and more or less vaguely related to Beowulf. Wexstan killed the older of Onela's nephews, when that Swedish king invaded Geatland, but whether he was himself a Swede, or a Geat serving the Swedes, is not known. In any case, after the survivor of Onela's two nephews returned to Sweden, killed Onela, and became king, Wexstan could not (and did not) remain in Sweden.

WIGLAF: a Geat warrior, more or less vaguely related to Beowulf, possibly having some Swedish blood; his father is Wexstan. Chosen to accompany Beowulf to the aged hero's fight with the dragon, Wiglaf is the only member of a presumably select band who goes to Beowulf's help. He seems to have become king, after Beowulf's death.

WULF: a Geat warrior, Efor's brother.

WULFGAR: Hrothgar's herald. The precise familial link which leads the poet to call him "a prince born to the Swedes."

WULFINGS: a Germanic tribe, probably resident south of the Baltic Sea. Welthow, Hrothgar's queen, may have been a Wulfing.

YRS: daughter of Healfdane. Her name is not actually given in the manuscript; despite the high degree of probability, editors have hesitated to fill the gap with anything more than [   ] and a footnote. A translator must either gamble or evade.

Related Readings

The New Beowulf

In this interview with Elizabeth Farnsworth, Seamus Heaney—poet, translator, and winner of the Nobel Prize for Literature—describes his fascination with the timeless story of Beowulf *and explains his own desire to translate this work.*

Elizabeth Farnsworth: A new translation of the epic poem "Beowulf" by the Irish poet Seamus Heaney is improbably on bestseller lists in several major U.S. cities, Los Angeles and San Francisco, among them. The poem was written in Old English more than 1,000 years ago. It tells the tale of the Scandinavian warrior, Beowulf, who slays two hellish demons and then in old age, brave beyond reason, is fatally wounded in a battle with a fiery dragon.

The poet and translator, Seamus Heaney, was born on a farm in Northern Ireland, and now divides his time between Dublin and teaching at Harvard University. He won the Nobel Prize for literature in 1995, for what the Nobel Committee described as "works of lyrical beauty and ethical depth, which exalt everyday miracles and the living past."

Thank you for being with us, Mr. Heaney.

Seamus Heaney, Poet/Translator, "Beowulf:" A pleasure.

EF: Those words from the Nobel Committee might describe "Beowulf," too, with its ethical concerns and the past so alive in it. Have you always had an affinity for "Beowulf"?

SH: Well, I read the poem when I was an undergraduate. I was actually made to read it as part of my English course. When I was in my teens, I actually knew the shorter Anglo-Saxon poems better, but "Beowulf" was the large, 3,000-line monster lying there at the very beginning of the tradition.

And the language it was written in and the meter it was written in attracted me, partly because, as I say in the introduction to the translation, I think there's something in the very sturdy, stressed nature of that old language that matched the speech I grew up with in Ulster, in the countryside in the 1940's.

EF: We don't know who wrote it. You're not even sure exactly when it was written, are you?

SH: No, it was written, as I said, towards the end of the first millennium, maybe in the 700's, maybe towards the year 1000, but that's not . . . we're not very sure about that. We do know that whoever wrote it lived in two worlds, in a way—lived in a past that belonged to the Old English ancestry, that is the people who came over from Jutland and the Angles and the Saxons and the Jutes, they came across the North Sea to England. So they brought memories of a Scandinavian past with them. So the poet is someone with . . . who lived in that previous, as they say "pagan" past. And he's also a Christian, someone who has taken in the new Mediterranean Christian culture. And the two voices, the two things are in the poem. The story is of the old, previous archaic material, and the understanding and the voice that speaks is someone who is in touch with the new Christian culture.

EF: And then how did you find the tone and the voice for your own translation? I read that a word, is it "polean," helped you.

SH: Yeah, well, this poem is written down, but it is also clearly a poem that was spoken out. And it is spoken in a very dignified, formal way. And I got the notion that the best voice I could hear it in was the voice of an old countryman who was a cousin of my father's who was not, as they say, educated, but he spoke with great dignity and formality. And I thought if I could write the translation in such a way that this man—Peter Scullion was his name—could speak it, then I would get it right. That's, in fact, how I started it.

EF: And you found words that had actually been words that you knew from childhood, right?

SH: Yeah, that's right. My aunt used a word. In fact, all the people around the district, in the countryside, use words that I gradually began to realize the more I read were Anglo-Saxon words. They would say, for example, of people who had suffered some bereavement[1] "well, they just have to thole." And they would say it to you when they're putting the poultice[2] on your hand that was burning, "You'll have to thole this, child." Now thole . . . "Thole" means "to suffer," but it's there in the glossaries of Anglo-Saxon, "tholian." So between the secret dialect speech of my home ground and the upper level discourse of the Anglo-Saxon textbook in university, there was this commerce. And I felt my own ear, my own language lived between . . . lived between that country-speak and learned-speak, and therefore, that I had some way of translating it, of carrying over from one to the other. I felt there was, like, a little passport into translating it, you know.

Poetry has no tense

EF: Would you read something for us, please?

SH: Yeah, I'll read a bit, one of my favorite little bits where it describes a poet in the Anglo-Saxon king's hall, a minstrel singing his poem, and the poem is a story of the creation of the world. And in this very . . . this very happy scene is surrounded by darkness where the monster is prowling, the monster called Grendel.

> Then a powerful demon, a prowler through the dark,
> nursed a hard grievance. It harrowed him
> to hear the din of the loud banquet
> every day in the hall, the harp being struck
> and the clear song of a skilled poet
> telling with mastery of man's beginnings,
> how the Almighty had made the earth
> a gleaming plain girdled with waters;
> in His splendour He set the sun and the moon
> to be earth's lamplight, lanterns for men,
> and filled the broad lap of the world
> with branches and leaves; and quickened life
> in every other thing that moved.

EF: Now read a little bit of it in Anglo-Saxon for us.

SH: Well, these are just a little, few lines at the beginning (speaking in Anglo-Saxon).

---

1. **bereavement** here, the loss of a loved one by death
2. **poultice** a warm medicated mass applied on cloth to a body sore

EF: The metrics of it, the balancing halves of the line, explain that, because it seems to be, at least for me, what kept pulling me through it.

SH: Yeah, well the line is in two halves. But there are two stresses and two stresses "telling with mastery of man's beginnings." "To be earth's lamplight, lanterns for men." "Then a powerful demon, a prowler through the dark." You've got the two stresses, but you will notice there's also a little loop from one half to the other of alliteration. "Powerful . . . prowler . . . / . . . a hard grievance. It harrowed him." "A gleaming plain girdled with waters." "Earth's lamplight, lanterns for men." The "l"s—"earth's lamplight, lanterns for men"—they end, then "the Almighty . . . made the earth." The "p"— "powerful demon, . . . prowler through the dark." So instead of rhyming, you have those different principles for repeating the pattern line by line right through.

EF: And the world of "Beowulf"—you referred to this earlier—but this old world, the warrior . . . the Germanic warrior culture that's evoked, which is honor-bound, blood-stained, vengeance-driven . . .

SH: Yeah.

EF: Did it seem particularly familiar to you? Was it like Ireland?

SH: Well, no. Ireland doesn't live by the sword and doesn't, I mean, we're in a kind of different cultural situation. We aren't commanded once somebody has killed to go out and kill someone else. That isn't the code. But it is true that the . . . that what does strike the contemporary reader of "Beowulf" is that that sense of small ethnic groups living together with memories of wrongs on each side, with a border between them that may be breached. I mean, after the breakup of the former Yugoslavia, after Bosnia and Kosovo and so on, the feuds between the Swedes and the Geats, these little dynastic, ethnic, furious battles strike a chord. Not, it's not just . . . I wouldn't say it was just in Northern Ireland, where there is of course an ethnic energy and a vengefulness from the past. But it's more widespread than that. And I say in the introduction and I think it's absolutely true, towards the end of the poem there's a scene, a funeral scene, where a woman begins to wail and weep with her hair bound up. And she cries out a chant of grief. And I think, instead of it being very far away, it's actually quite close now— through paradoxically all the modern technological means of television, which bring us newsreels of sorrow right into the drawing room. And that figure of the woman wailing because of grief, because of atrocity, it's quite familiar and very close. And the poem, I would say, is fit for this kind of atrocious reality. The poet understands—he has a veteran's understanding—that the world is not quite trustworthy and that we must be grateful for it when it is trustworthy.

EF: And finally, Mr. Heaney, how do you explain the fact that "Beowulf," this old, old poem with its old, old code is so popular right now? I mean, it's number seven on the "San Francisco Chronicle" bestseller list. It's number three, I think, in Los Angeles.

SH: Well, I'm glad to hear that. I think poetry has no tense, you know, past or present. The reality that it deals with is kind of the . . . what our consciousness contains and what, how we are fit for reality. And when you get something like "Beowulf" or something like Homer, then you're dealing with the clear, present reality of human understanding and human action, and as I say, it's so true that the tense of past or present doesn't enter. It is the truthfulness of the representation of the kind of creatures we are, I think.

EF: Seamus Heaney, thank you very much for being with us.

SH: Thank you.

from
Grendel

John Gardner

Told from the point of view of the monster, the novel
Grendel pokes fun at the uncivilized behavior of humans.
In Chapters 11 and 12, Grendel battles with the young
accomplished hero, Beowulf.

11

I AM MAD WITH JOY—At least I think it's joy. Strangers have come, and
it's a whole new game. I kiss the ice on the frozen creeks, I press my ear to it,
honoring the water that rattles below, for by water they came: the icebergs
parted as if gently pushed back by enormous hands, and the ship sailed
through, sea-eager, foamy-necked, white sails riding the swan-road, flying
like a bird! O happy Grendel! Fifteen glorious heroes, proud in their battle
dress, fat as cows!

I could feel them coming as I lay in the dark of my cave. I stirred, baffled
by the strange sensation, squinting into dark corners to learn the cause. It
drew me as the mind of the dragon did once. *It's coming!* I said. More clearly
than ever I heard the muffled footsteps on the dome of the world, and even
when I realized that the footsteps were nothing but the sound of my own
heart, I knew more surely than before that something was coming. I got up,
moved past stone icicles to the pool and the sunken door. My mother made
no move to prevent me. At the pool, firesnakes shot away from me in all di-
rections, bristling, hissing, mysteriously wrought up. They had sensed it too.
That beat—steady, inhumanly steady; inexorable.[1] And so, an hour before
dawn, I crouched in shadows at the rocky sea-wall, foot of the giants' work.
Low tide. Lead-gray water sucked quietly, stubborn and deliberate, at icy
gray boulders. Gray wind teased leafless trees. There was no sound but the
ice-cold surge, the cry of a gannet,[2] invisible in grayness above me. A whale
passed, long dark shadow two miles out. The sky grew light at my back.
Then I saw the sail.

---

1. **inexorable** relentless
2. **gannet** large sea bird

I was not the only one who saw them coming. A lone Danish coastguard stood bundled in furs, his horse beside him, and he shaded his eyes against the glint of the icebergs beyond the sail and watched the strangers come swiftly in toward land. The wooden keel struck sand and cut a gouge toward the boulders on the shore—a forty-foot cut, half the length of the ship—and then, quick as wolves—but mechanical, terrible—the strangers leaped down, and with stiff, ice-crusted ropes as gray as the sea, the sky, the stones, they moored their craft. Their chain-mail rattled as they worked—never speaking, walking dead men—lashing the helm-bar, lowering the sail, unloading ashspear shafts and battle-axes. The coastguard mounted, snatched up his spear, and rode loudly down to meet them. His horse's hooves shot sparks. I laughed. If they were here for war, the coastguard was a goner.

"What are ye, bearers of armor, dressed in mailcoats, that have thus come riding your tall ship over the searoad, winter-cold ocean, here to Daneland?" Thus spake the coastguard. Wind took his words and sent them tumbling.

I bent double, soundlessly laughing till I thought I'd split. They were like trees, these strangers. Their leader was big as a mountain, moving with his forest toward the guard. Nevertheless, the Dane shook his spear. . . . "Attaboy!" I whisper. I shadow box. "If they come at you, bite 'em in the leg!"

He scolded and fumed and demanded their lineage; they listened with folded arms. The wind blew colder. At last the coastguard's voice gave out—he bent over the pommel, coughing into his fist—and the leader answered. His voice, though powerful, was mild. Voice of a dead thing, calm as dry sticks and ice when the wind blows over them. He had a strange face that, little by little grew unsettling to me: it was a face, or so it seemed for an instant, from a dream I had almost forgotten. The eyes slanted downward, never blinking, unfeeling as a snake's. He had no more beard than a fish. He smiled as he spoke, but it was as if the gentle voice, the childlike yet faintly ironic smile were holding something back, some magician-power that could blast stone cliffs to ashes as lightning blasts trees.

"We're Geats," he said, "the hearth-companions of King Hygilac. You've heard of my father. A famous old man named Egtheow." His mind, as he spoke, seemed far away, as if, though polite, he were indifferent to all this— an outsider not only among the Danes but everywhere. He said: "We've come as friends for a visit with your lord King Hrothgar, protector of the people." He tipped his head, pausing. You'd have thought he had centuries. At last with a little shrug, he said, "Be so kind as to give us some advice, old man. We've come on a fairly important errand." The hint of irony in the smile grew darker, and he looked now not at the coastguard but at the coast-guard's horse. "A certain thing can't very well be kept hidden, I think. You'll know if it's true, as we heard back home, that I don't know what kind of enemy stalks your hall at night—kills men, so they say, and for some reason scorns your warriors. If it's so—" He paused, his eyebrows cocked, and glanced at the coastguard and smiled, "I've come to give Hrothgar advice."

You could see pretty well what advice he'd give. His chest was as wide as an oven. His arms were like beams. "Come ahead," I whispered. "Make your play. Do your worst." But I was less sure of myself than I pretended. Staring at his grotesquely muscled shoulders—stooped, naked despite the cold, sleek as the belly of a shark and as rippled with power as the shoulders of a horse—I found my mind wandering. If I let myself, I could drop into a trance just looking at those shoulders. He was dangerous. And yet I was excited, suddenly alive. He talked on. I found myself not listening, merely looking at his mouth, which moved—or so it seemed to me—independent of the words, as if the body of the stranger were a ruse, a disguise for something infinitely more terrible. Then the coastguard turned his horse and led them up to where the stone-paved road began, gray as the sea, between snowbanks. "I'll have men guard your ship," he said. He pointed out the meadhall, high on its hill above the town. Then he turned back. The sea-pale eyes of the stranger were focused on nothing. He and his company went on, their weapons clinking, chain-mail jangling, solemn and ominous as drums. They moved like one creature, huge strange machine. Sunlight gleamed on their helmets and cheekguards and flashed off their spearpoints, blinding. I did not follow. I stayed in the ruin, prowling where long-dead giants prowled, my heart aching to know what the strangers were doing now, up at the meadhall. But it was daylight; I'd be a fool to go up and see.

I couldn't tell, back in my cave, whether I was afraid of them or not. My head ached from staying too long in the sunlight, and my hands had no grip. It was as if they were asleep. I was unnaturally conscious, for some reason, of the sounds in the cave: the roar of the underground river hundreds of feet below our rooms, reaming out walls, driving deeper and deeper; the centuries-old drip-drip of seepage building stalagmites, an inch in a hundred years; the spatter of the spring three rooms away—the room of the pictures half buried in stone—where the spring breaks through the roof. Half awake, half asleep, I felt as if I were myself the cave, my thoughts coursing downward through my own strange hollows . . . or some impulse older and darker than thought, as old as the mindless mechanics of a bear, the twilight meditations of a wolf, a tree . . .

Who knows what all this means? Neither awake nor asleep, my chest filled with an excitement like joy, I tried to think whether or not I was afraid of the strangers, and the thought made no sense. It was unreal—insubstantial as spiderweb-strands blowing lightly across a window that looks out on trees. I have sometimes watched men do mysterious things. A man with a wife and seven children, a carpenter with a fair reputation as wise, not maddened by passions, not given to foolishness—regular of habit, dignified in bearing, a dedicated craftsman (no edge unbeveled, no ragged peg, no gouge or split)— once crept from his house at the edge of the town while his family slept, and fled down snowy paths through woods to the house of a hunter away in search of game. The hunter's wife admitted him, and he slept with her until the second rooster crowed then he fled back home. Who knows why? Tedium is the worst pain. The mind lays out the world in blocks, and the hushed blood waits for revenge. All order, I've come to understand, is theoretical, unreal—a harmless, sensible, smiling mask men slide between the two great, dark realities, the self and the world—two snake-pits. The watchful mind lies, cunning and swift, about the dark blood's lust, lies and lies and lies until, weary of talk, the watchman sleeps. Then sudden and swift the enemy strikes from nowhere, the cavernous heart. Violence is truth, as the crazy old peasant told Hrothulf. But the old fool only half grasped what he said. He had never conversed with a dragon. And the stranger?

Afraid or not, I would go to the meadhall, I knew. I toyed, of course, with the ridiculous theory that I'd stay where I was safe, like a sensible beast. "Am I not free?—as free as a bird?" I whispered, leering, maniacal. I have seen—I embody—the vision of the dragon: absolute, final waste. I saw long ago the whole universe as not-my-mother, and I glimpsed my place in it, a hole. *Yet I exist*, I knew. *Then I alone exist*, I said. *It's me or it.* What glee, that glorious recognition! (The cave my cave is a jealous cave.) For even my mama loves me not for myself, my holy specialness (he he ho ha), but for my son-ness, my possessedness, my displacement of air as visible proof of her power. I have set her aside—gently, picking her up by the armpits as I would a child—and so have proved that she has no power but the little I give her by momentary whim. So I might set aside Hrothgar's whole kingdom and all his thanes[3] if I did not, for sweet desire's sake, set limits to desire. If I murdered the last of the Scyldings,[4] what would I live for? I'd have to move.

So now, for once unsure of victory, I might set limits to desire: go to sleep, put off further raids till the Geats go home. For the world is divided, experience teaches, into two parts: things to be murdered, and things that would hinder the murder of things: and the Geats might reasonably be defined either way. So I whispered, wading through drifts waist-high, inexorably on my way to Hrothgar's meadhall. Darkness lay over the world like a coffin lid. I hurried. It would be a shame to miss the boasting. I came to the hall, bent down at my chink, peered in. The wind was shrill, full of patterns.

---

3. **thanes** in Anglo Saxon culture, warriors bound by vows of loyalty to fight for their lord, who, in return, was expected to reward and protect them

4. **Scyldings** (shild' ings) the descendants of Shild, a Danish king; the Danes

It was a scene to warm the cockles of your heart. The Danes were not pleased, to say the least, that the Geats had come to save them. Honor is very big with them; they'd rather be eaten alive than be bailed out by strangers. The priests weren't happy either. They'd been saying for years that the ghostly Destroyer would take care of things in time. Now here were these foreigner upstarts unmasking religion! My old friend Ork sat shaking his head in dismay, saying nothing, brooding, no doubt, on the dark metaphysical implications. Things fade; alternatives exclude. Whichever of us might exclude the other, when the time came for me and the stranger to meet, the eyes of the people would be drawn to the instance, they would fail to rise to the holy idea of process. Theology does not thrive in the world of action and reaction, change: it grows on calm, like the scum on a stagnant pool. And it flourishes, it prospers, on decline. Only in a world where everything is patently being lost can a priest stir men's hearts as a poet would by maintaining that nothing is in vain. For old times' sake, for the old priest's honor, I would have to kill the stranger. And for the honor of Hrothgar's thanes.

The Danes sat sulking, watching the strangers eat, wishing some one of them would give them an excuse to use their daggers. I covered my mouth to keep from cackling. The king presided, solemn and irritable. He knew that his thanes couldn't handle me alone, and he was too old and tired to be much impressed—however useful it might be to his kingdom—by their fathead ideas of honor. *Get through the meal, that's the thing,* he was thinking. *Keep them from wasting their much touted skills on one another.* The queen wasn't present. Situation much too touchy.

Then up spoke Unferth, Ecglaf's son, top man in Hrothgar's hall. He had a nose like a black, deformed potato, eyes like a couple of fangs. He leaned forward over the table and pointed the dagger he'd been eating with. "Say, friend," he said to the beardless leader of the Geats, "are you the same man that went swimming that time with young Breca—risked your lives in the middle of the winter for nothing—for a crazy meadboast?"

The stranger stopped eating, smiled.

"We heard about that," Unferth said. "Nobody could stop you—kings, priests, councilors—nobody. Splash! *Uh, uh, uh!*" Unferth made swimming motions, eyes rolled up, mouth gasping. The thanes around him laughed. "The sea boiled with waves, fierce winter swells. Seven nights you swam, so people say." He made his face credulous, and the Danes laughed again. "And at last Breca beat you, much stronger than you were. He proved his boast against you—for what it may be worth." The Danish thanes laughed. Even Hrothgar smiled. Unferth grew serious, and now only the stranger went on smiling, he alone and the huge Geats next to him, patient as timberwolves. Unferth pointed with his dagger, giving friendly advice. "I predict it will go

FROM GRENDEL **109**

even worse for you tonight. You may have had successes—I haven't heard. But wait up for Grendel for one night's space and all your glorious successes will be done with."

The Danes applauded. The stranger smiled on, his downward-slanting eyes like empty pits. I could see his mind working, stone-cold, grinding like a millwheel. When the hall was still, he spoke, soft-voiced, his weird gaze focused nowhere. "Ah, friend Unferth, drunk with mead you've said a good deal about Breca. The truth is, nevertheless, that I beat him. I'm stronger in the ocean than any other man alive. Like foolish boys we agreed on the match and boasted, yes . . . we were both very young . . . swore we'd risk our lives in the sea, and did so. We took swords with us, swimming one-handed, to fight off whales."

Unferth laughed, and the others followed, as was right. It was preposterous.

The stranger said, "Breca couldn't swim away from me, for all his strength—a man with arms like yours, friend Unferth—and as for myself, I chose not to swim away from him. Thus we swam for five nights, and then a storm came up, icy wind from the north, black sky, raging waves, and we were separated. The turmoil stirred up the sea-monsters. One of them attacked me, dragged me down to the bottom where the weight of the sea would have crushed any other man. But it was granted to me that I might kill him with my sword, which same I did. Then others attacked. They pressed me hard. I killed them, nine old water nickers, robbed them of the feast they expected at the bottom of the sea. In the morning, sword-ripped, they lay belly-up near shore. They'd trouble no more passing sailors after that. Light came from the east and, behold, I saw headlands, and I swam to them. Fate often enough will spare a man if his courage holds."

Now the Danes weren't laughing. The stranger said it all so calmly, so softly, that it was impossible to laugh. He believed every word he said. I understood at last the look in his eyes. He was insane.

Even so, I wasn't prepared for what came next. Nobody was. Solemn, humorless despite the slightly ironic smile, he suddenly cut deep—yet with the same mildness, the same almost inhuman indifference except for the pale flash of fire in his eyes. "Neither Breca nor you ever fought such battles," he said. "I don't boast much of that. Nevertheless, I don't recall hearing any glorious deeds of yours, except that you murdered your brothers. You'll prowl the stalagmites of hell for that, friend Unferth—clever though you are."

The hall was numb. The stranger was no player of games.

And yet he was shrewd, you had to grant. Whether or not they believed his wild tale of superhuman strength, no thane in the hall would attack him again and risk the slash of that mild, coolly murderous tongue.

Old King Hrothgar, for one, was pleased. The madman's single-mindedness would be useful in a monster fight. He spoke: "Where's the queen? We're all friends in this hall! Let her come to us and pass the bowl!"

She must have been listening behind her door. She came out, radiant, and crossed swiftly to the great golden bowl on the table by the hearth. As if she'd brought light and warmth with her, men began talking, joking, laughing, both Danes and Geats together. When she'd served all the Danes and the lesser Geats, she stood, red hair flowing, her neck and arms adorned in gold, by the leader of the strangers. "I thank God," she said, "that my wish has been granted, that at last I have found a man whose courage I can trust."

The stranger smiled, glanced at Unferth. Hrothgar's top man had recovered a little, though his neck was still dark red.

"We'll see," the stranger said.

And again I found something peculiar happening to my mind. His mouth did not seem to move with his words, and the harder I stared at his gleaming shoulders, the more uncertain I was of their shape. The room was full of a heavy, unpleasant scent I couldn't place. I labor to remember something: twisted roots, an abyss . . . I lose it. The queer little spasm of terror passes. Except for his curious beardlessness, there is nothing frightening about the stranger. I've broken the backs of bulls no weaker than he is.

Hrothgar made speeches, his hand on the queen's. Unferth sat perfectly still, no longer blushing. He was struggling to make himself hope for the stranger's success, no doubt. *Heroism is more than noble language, dignity. Inner heroism, that's the trick! Glorious carbuncle of the soul! Except in the life of the hero the whole world's meaningless.* He took a deep breath. He would try to be a better person, yes. He forced a smile, but it twisted, out of his control. Tears! He got up suddenly and, without a word, walked out.

Hrothgar told the hall that the stranger was like a son to him. The queen's smile was distant, and the nephew, Hrothulf, picked at the table with a dirty fingernail. "You already have more sons than you need," the queen laughed lightly. Hrothgar laughed too, though he didn't seem to get it. He was tipsy. The stranger went on sitting with the same unlighted smile. The old king chatted of his plans for Freawaru, how he would marry her off to his enemy, the king of the Heathobards. The stranger smiled on, but closed his eyes. He knew a doomed house when he saw it, I had a feeling; but for one reason or another he kept his peace. I grew more and more afraid of him and at the same time—who can explain it?—more and more eager for the hour of our meeting.

The queen rose, at last, and retired. The fire in the hearth had now died down. The priests filed out to the god-ring to do their devotions. Nobody followed. I could hear them in the distance: "O ghostly Destroyer . . ." The cold ring of gods stared inward with large, dead eyes.

It is the business of rams to be rams and of goats to be goats, the business of shapers to sing and of kings to rule. The stranger waits on, as patient as a grave-mound. I too wait, whispering, whispering, mad like him. Time grows, obeying its mechanics, like all of us. So the young Shaper observes, singing to the few who remain, fingertips troubling a dead man's harp.

> *Frost shall freeze, and fire melt wood;*
> *the earth shall give fruit, and ice shall bridge*
> *dark water, make roofs, mysteriously lock*
> *earth's flourishings; but the fetters of frost*
> *shall also fall, fair weather return,*
> *and the reaching sun restore the restless sea. . . .*

We wait.
The King retires, and his people leave.
The Geats build up the fire, prepare to sleep.
And now, silence.
Darkness.
It is time.

12

I touch the door with my fingertips and it bursts, for all its fire-forged bands—it jumps away like a terrified deer—and I plunge into the silent, hearthlit hall with a laugh that I wouldn't much care to wake up to myself. I trample the planks that a moment before protected the hall like a hand raised in horror to a terrified mouth (sheer poetry, ah!) and the broken hinges rattle like swords down the timbered walls. The Geats are stones, and whether it's because they're numb with terror or stiff from too much mead, I cannot tell. I am swollen with excitement, bloodlust and joy and a strange fear that mingle in my chest like the twisting rage of a bone-fire. I step onto the brightly shining floor and angrily advance on them. They're all asleep, the whole company! I can hardly believe my luck and my wild heart laughs, but I let out no sound. Swiftly, softly, I will move from bed to bed and destroy them all, swallow every last man. I am blazing, half-crazy with joy. For pure, mad prank, I snatch a cloth from the nearest table and tie it around my neck to make a napkin. I delay no longer. I seize up a sleeping man, tear at him hungrily, bite through his bone-locks and suck hot, slippery blood. He goes down in huge morsels, head, chest, hips, legs, even the hands and feet. My face and arms are wet, matted. The napkin is sopping. The dark floor steams. I move on at once and I reach for another one (whispering, whispering, chewing the universe down to words), and I seize a wrist. A shock goes through me. Mistake!

It's a trick! His eyes are open, were open all the time, cold-bloodedly watching to see how I work. The eyes nail me now as his hand nails down my arm. I jump back without thinking (whispering wildly: *jump back without thinking*). Now he's out of his bed, his hand still closed like a dragon's jaws on mine. Nowhere on middle-earth, I realize, have I encountered a grip like his. My whole arm's on fire, incredible, searing pain—it's as if his crushing fingers are charged like fangs with poison. I scream, facing him, grotesquely shaking hands—dear long-lost brother, kinsman-thane—and the timbered hall screams back at me. I feel the bones go, ground from their sockets, and I scream again. I am suddenly awake. The long pale dream, my history, falls away. The meadhall is alive, great cavernous[5] belly, gold-adorned, blood-stained, howling back at me, lit by the flickering fire in the stranger's eyes. He has wings. Is it possible? And yet it's true: out of his shoulders come terrible fiery wings. I jerk my head, trying to drive out illusion. The world is what it is and always was. That's our hope, our chance. Yet even in times of catastrophe we people it with tricks. Grendel, Grendel, hold fast to what is true!

---

5. **cavernous** like a large cave

Suddenly, darkness. My sanity has won. He's only a man; I can escape him. I plan. I feel the plan moving inside me like thaw-time waters rising between cliffs. When I'm ready, I give a ferocious kick—but something's wrong: I am spinning—*Wa!*—falling through bottomless space—*Wa!*—snatching at the huge twisted roots of an oak . . . a blinding flash of fire . . . no, darkness. I concentrate. I have fallen! Slipped on blood. He viciously twists my arm behind my back. By accident, it comes to me, I have given him a greater advantage. I could laugh. *Woe, woe!*

And now something worse. He's whispering—spilling words like showers of sleet, his mouth three inches from my ear. I will not listen. I continue whispering. As long as I whisper myself I need not hear. His syllables lick at me, chilly fire. His syllables lick at me, chilly fire. His syllables lick at me, chilly fire. His syllables lick . . .

Grendel, Grendel! You make the world by whispers, second by second. Are you blind to that? Whether you make it a grave or a garden of roses is not the point. Feel the wall: is it not hard? He smashes me against it, breaks open my forehead. *Hard, yes! Observe the hardness, write it down in careful runes. Now sing of walls! Sing!*

I howl.

Sing!

"I'm singing!"

Sing words! Sing raving hymns!

"You're crazy. Ow!"

Sing!

"I sing of walls," I howl. "Hooray for the hardness of walls!"

Terrible, he whispers. *Terrible*. He laughs and lets out fire.

"You're crazy," I say. "If you think I created that wall that cracked my head, you're a . . . lunatic."

Sing walls, he hisses.

I have no choice.

"The wall will fall to the wind as the windy hill
will fall, and all things thought in former times:
Nothing made remains, nor man remembers.
And these towns shall be called the shining towns!"

Better, he whispers. *That's better.* He laughs again, and the nasty laugh admits I'm slyer than he guessed.

He's crazy. I understand him all right, make no mistake. Understand his lunatic theory of matter and mind, the chilly intellect, the hot imagination, blocks and builder, reality as stress. Nevertheless, it was by accident that he got my arm behind me. He penetrated no mysteries. He was lucky. If I'd known he was awake, if I'd known there was blood on the floor when I gave him that kick . . .

The room goes suddenly white, as if struck by lightning. I stare down, amazed. He has torn off my arm at the shoulder! Blood pours down where the limb was. I cry, I bawl like a baby. He stretches his blinding white wings and breathes out fire. I run for the door and through it. I move like wind. I stumble and fall, get up again. I'll die! I howl. The night is aflame with winged men. *No, no! Think!* I come suddenly awake once more from the nightmare. Darkness. I really will die! Every rock, every tree, every crystal of snow cries out cold-blooded objectness. Cold, sharp outlines, everything around me: distinct, detached as dead men. I understand. "Mama!" I bellow. "Mama, Mama! I'm dying!" But her love is history. His whispering follows me into the woods, though I've outrun him. "It was an accident," I bellow back. I will cling to what is true. "Blind, mindless, mechanical. Mere logic of chance." I am weak from loss of blood. No one follows me now. I stumble again and with my one weak arm I cling to the huge twisted roots of an oak. I look down past stars to a terrifying darkness. I seem to recognize the place, but it's impossible. "Accident," I whisper. I will fall. I seem to desire the fall, and though I fight it with all my will I know in advance that I can't win. Standing baffled, quaking with fear, three feet from the edge of a nightmare cliff, I find myself, incredibly, moving toward it. I look down, down, into bottomless blackness, feeling the dark power moving in me like an ocean current, some monster inside me, deep sea wonder, dread night monarch astir in his cave, moving me slowly to my voluntary tumble into death.

Again sight clears. I am slick with blood. I discover I no longer feel pain. Animals gather around me, enemies of old, to watch me die. I give them what I hope will appear a sheepish smile. My heart booms terror. Will the last of my life slide out if I let out breath? They watch with mindless, indifferent eyes, as calm and midnight black as the chasm below me.

Is it joy I feel?

They watch on, evil, incredibly stupid, enjoying my destruction.

"Poor Grendel's had an accident," I whisper. *"So may you all."*

Translated by
Charles W. Kennedy

Old English Riddles

*Creating and guessing riddles were popular intellectual
activities during Anglo-Saxon times. These riddles were
originally written in Old English, sometime between the
seventh and eleventh centuries.*

Oft I must strive   with wind and wave,
Battle them both   when under the sea
I feel out the bottom,   a foreign land.
In lying still   I am strong in the strife;
5   If I fail in that   they are stronger than I
And, wrenching me loose,   soon put me to rout.
They wish to capture   what I must keep.
I can master them both   if my grip holds out,
If the rocks bring succor° and lend support,
10   Strength in the struggle.   Ask me my name!

My house is not quiet,   I am not loud;
But for us God fashioned   our fate together.
I am the swifter,   at times the stronger,
My house more enduring,   longer to last.
At times I rest;   my dwelling still runs;
Within it I lodge   as long as I live.
Should we two be severed,   my death is sure.

---

9. **succor** aid, relief

A lonely wanderer,   wounded with iron,
I am smitten with war-blades,   sated° with strife,
Worn with the sword-edge;   I have seen many
    battles,
Much hazardous fighting,   oft without hope
5   Of comfort or help   in the carnage of war
Ere I perish and fall   in the fighting of men.
The leavings of hammers,   the handwork of smiths,
Batter and bite me,   hard-edged and sharp;
The brunt of battle   I am doomed to endure.
10   In all the folk-stead   no leech could I find
With wort or simple   to heal my wounds;
But day and night   with the deadly blows
The marks of the war-blades   double and deepen.

---

2. sated supplied with more than enough; glutted

The Slaying of the Dragon

Dino Buzzati

A scientific expedition in search of a legendary dragon takes five Italians high up into the mountains.

In MAY 1902 A PEASANT IN THE SERVICE of Count Gerol, one Giosue Longo, who often went hunting in the mountains, reported that he had seen a large animal, resembling a dragon, in Valle Secca. Palissano, the last village in the valley, had long cherished a legend that one such monster was still living in certain arid passes in the region. But no one had ever taken it seriously. Yet on this one occasion Longo's obvious sanity, the exactitude of his account, the absolutely accurate and unwavering repetition of details of the event convinced people that there might be something in it, and Count Martino Gerol decided to go and find out. Naturally he was not thinking in terms of a dragon; but it was possible that there was some huge, rare serpent still living in those uninhabited valleys.

He was to be accompanied on the expedition by the governor of the province, Quinto Andronico, and his beautiful and intrepid[1] wife, Maria, the naturalist Professor Inghirami, and his colleague Fusti, who was an expert in taxidermy. Quinto Andronico was a weak, skeptical man and had known for some time that his wife was attracted to Count Gerol, but this did not worry him. In fact, he agreed willingly when Maria suggested that they should accompany the count on his hunt. He was not the least bit jealous, nor even envious, although Gerol was greatly superior to him in wealth, youth, good looks, strength, and courage.

Two carriages left the town shortly after midnight with an escort of eight mounted hunters and arrived at Palissano at about six the following morning. Gerol, Maria, and the two naturalists slept. Only Andronico remained awake, and he stopped the carriage in front of the house of an old friend of his, the doctor Taddei. After a few moments the doctor, still half asleep, appeared at a second-floor window. Andronico greeted him jovially from

---

1. **intrepid** outstandingly courageous

below and explained the object of the expedition, expecting his listener to burst out laughing at the mention of dragons. To his surprise, Taddei shook his head disapprovingly.

"I wouldn't go if I were you," he said firmly.

"Why not? Don't you think it's a lot of nonsense?"

"No," the doctor replied. "Personally I think there is a dragon, though I've never seen it."

"Do you mean you really believe in the dragon?"

"I'm an old man," said the doctor, "and I've seen many things. It may be a lot of nonsense, but it may also be true. If I were you, I wouldn't get involved. The way is hard to find, the rocks are unsafe, and there isn't a drop of water. Why not go down to the Crocetta? You'll find plenty of hares there." He was silent for a moment, then added: "I assure you, I wouldn't go. I once heard it said—but you'll only laugh."

"I won't laugh." Andronico protested. "Please go on."

"Well, some people say that this dragon gives out smoke, and that it's poisonous and a small quantity can kill you."

Forgetting his promise, Andronico laughed loudly. "I always knew you were eccentric," he snorted. "But this is too much. You're medieval, my dear Taddei. I'll see you this evening, and I'll be sporting a dragon's head."

He waved good-bye, climbed back into the carriage, and ordered the coach to move on. Giosue Longo, who was one of the hunters and knew the way, went to the head of the convoy.

"What was that old man shaking his head at?" asked Maria, who was now awake.

"Nothing," Andronico said. "It was only old Taddei, who's an amateur vet. We were talking about foot-and-mouth disease."

"And the dragon?" asked Count Gerol, who was sitting opposite him. "Did you ask him about the dragon?"

"No, I didn't, to be quite honest," said Andronico. "I didn't want to be laughed at. I told him we'd come up here to do a bit of hunting."

The passengers felt their weariness vanish as the sun rose. The horses moved faster, and the coachmen began to hum.

"Taddei used to be our family doctor," Andronico said. "Once he had a fashionable practice. Then he suddenly retired and went to live in the country, perhaps because of some disappointment in love. Then he must have experienced some kind of misfortune, for he came to this out-of-the-way place. Soon he'll be something of a dragon himself."

"What nonsense," said Maria, annoyed. "Always talking about the dragon. It's really becoming boring."

"It was your idea to come," said her husband, mildly amused.

Maria did not reply but looked worriedly at the mountains, which were becoming higher, steeper, and more arid. At the far end of the valley there appeared a chaotic succession of peaks, mostly conical and bare of woods or meadows, yellowish in color and terribly bleak. The scorching sunlight clothed them in a hard, strong light.

It was about nine o'clock when the carriages came to a standstill because the road came to an end. As the passengers climbed down, they realized they were now in the heart of those sinister mountains.

"Look, this is where the path starts," said Longo, pointing to a trail of footsteps leading upward toward the mouth of a small valley, which led to an amphitheater, where the dragon had been seen.

"Did you bring some water?" Andronico asked the hunters.

"There are four flasks of water and two of wine, your Excellency," one of them said.

"That should be enough."

Odd. Now that they were so far from the town, locked in the mountains, the idea of the dragon began to seem less absurd. The travelers looked around them and saw no signs of anything reassuring—only complete desolation.

They walked without speaking. First went the hunters with the guns, cannon, and other hunting equipment, then Count Gerol, Maria, Andronico, and finally the two naturalists.

At a certain point a young man appeared below them, walking faster than the hunting party and with a dead goat slung over his shoulders.

"He's going to the dragon," Longo said, as if it were the most natural thing in the world. The inhabitants of Palissano, he explained, were highly superstitious and sent a goat to the amphitheater every morning to placate[2] the monster. The young men of the region took turns taking the offering. If the dragon was heard to roar, this portended untold disaster; all kinds of misfortunes might follow.

"And the dragon eats the goat every day?" joked Count Gerol.

"There's nothing left of it the next day, that's certain."

"Not even the bones?"

"Not even the bones. It takes the goat into the cave to eat it."

"But couldn't it be someone from the village who eats the goat?" Andronico asked. "Everyone knows the way. Has anyone actually seen the dragon take the goat?"

"I don't know, your Excellency," replied the hunter.

Meanwhile, the young man with the goat had caught up with them.

---

2. **placate** to soothe the anger or hostility of

"Hey there, young man," Count Gerol called in his usual stentorian[3] manner, "how much do you want for that goat?"

"I can't sell it, sir."

"Not even for ten crowns?"

"Well, I could go and get another one, I suppose. For ten crowns . . ."

"What do you want the goat for?" Andronico asked. "Not to eat, I trust."

"You'll see in good time," Gerol said evasively.

One of the hunters put the goat over his shoulders, the young man headed back to the village to get another goat, and the hunting party moved off again.

After another hour's journey, they finally arrived. The valley suddenly opened out into a vast, rugged amphitheater surrounded by crumbling walls of orange-colored earth and rock. Right in the center, on top of a cone-shaped heap of debris, was a dark opening: the dragon's cave.

"That's it," said Longo.

They stopped quite near it, on a gravelly terrace which offered an excellent observation point, about thirty feet above the level of the cave and almost directly in front of it. The terrace had the added advantage of not being accessible from below because it stood at the top of an almost vertical wall.

They were all quiet, listening hard, but they could hear nothing except the endless silence of the mountains, broken by the occasional swish of gravel. Here and there lumps of earth would give way suddenly, streams of pebbles would pour down the mountainside and die down again gradually. The whole countryside seemed to be in a state of dilapidation, as if these mountains had been abandoned by their creator, being allowed to fall quietly to pieces.

"What if the dragon doesn't come out today?" Andronico asked.

"I've got the goat," Gerol said. "You seem to forget that."

Then they understood. The animal would act as bait to entice the dragon out of its lair.

They began their preparations. Two hunters struggled up to a height of about twenty yards above the entrance to the cave, to be able to hurl down stones if necessary. Another placed the goat on the gravelly expanse outside the cave. Others were posted on either side, well-protected by large stones, with the cannons and guns. Andronico stayed where he was, intending to remain a spectator.

Maria was silent. Her former boldness had vanished altogether. Although she wouldn't admit it, she would have given anything to be able to go back. She looked around at the walls of rock, at the scars of old

---

3. **stentorian** extremely loud

landslides and the debris of recent ones, at the pillars of red earth, which looked to her as though they might collapse any minute. Her husband, Count Gerol, the two naturalists, and the hunters seemed negligible protection in the face of such desolation.

When the dead goat had been placed in front of the cave, they began to wait. It was shortly after ten o'clock and the sun now infiltrated every crevice in the amphitheater, filling it with intense heat. Waves of heat were reflected back from one side to another. The hunters organized a rough canopy with the carriage covers for Andronico and Maria, to shield them from the sun.

"Watch out!" Count Gerol suddenly shouted from his vantage on a rock down near the cave, where he stood with a rifle in his hand and an iron club hanging from his hip.

A shudder went through the company as a live creature emerged from the mouth of the cave.

"The dragon!" shouted several of the hunters, though whether in joy or terror it was not clear.

The creature moved into the light with the hesitant sway of a snake. So here it was, this legendary monster whose voice made a whole village quake.

"How horrible!" Maria exclaimed with evident relief, having expected something far worse.

"Come on, courage!" shouted one of the hunters jokingly. Everyone became self-assured once again.

"It looks like a small Ceratosaurus!" said Professor Inghirami, now sufficiently confident to turn to the problems of science.

The monster wasn't really very terrible. It was little more than six feet long, with a head like a crocodile's, only shorter, a long lizardlike neck, a rather swollen thorax, a short tail, and a floppy sort of crest along its back. But its awkward movements, its clayey parchment color (with an occasional green streak here and there), and the apparent flabbiness of its body were even more reassuring than its small dimensions. The general impression was one of extreme age. If it was a dragon, it was a decrepit dragon, possibly moribund.[4]

"Take that!" scoffed one of the hunters who had climbed above the mouth of the cave. And he threw a rock down at the animal.

It hit the dragon on the skull. There was a hollow "tock," like the sound of something hitting a gourd. Maria felt a wave of revulsion.

The blow had been hard but not sufficient. The reptile was still for a few moments, as though stunned, and then began to shake its head from side to

---

4. **moribund** approaching death

side as if in pain. It opened and closed its jaws to reveal a set of sharp teeth, but it made no sound. Then it moved across the gravel toward the goat.

"Made you giddy, eh?" cackled Count Gerol, suddenly abandoning his arrogant pose. He seemed eager and excited in anticipation of the massacre.

A shot from the cannon, from a distance of about thirty yards, missed its mark. The explosion tore the stagnant air; the rock faces howled with the echo, setting in motion innumerable diminutive[5] landslides.

There was a second shot almost immediately. The bullet hit the animal on one of its back legs, producing a stream of blood.

"Look at it leaping around!" exclaimed Maria. She too was now enthralled by this show of cruelty. In the agony of its wound the animal had started to jump about in anguished circles. It drew its shattered leg after it, leaving a trail of black liquid on the gravel.

At last the reptile managed to reach the goat and to seize it in its teeth. It was about to turn around when Gerol, to advertise his own daring, went right up to it and shot it in the head from about six feet away.

A sort of whistling sound came from its jaws. It was as though it were trying to control itself, to repress its anger, to make as little noise as possible. The bullet from the rifle had hit it in the eye. After firing the shot, Count Gerol drew back and waited for it to collapse. But it didn't collapse; the spark of life within it seemed as persistent as a fire fed by pitch. The ball of lead lodged firmly in its eye, the monster calmly proceeded to devour the goat, and its neck swelled like rubber as the gigantic mouthfuls went down. Then it went back to the foot of the rocks and began to climb up the rock face beside the cave. It climbed with difficulty, as the earth kept giving way beneath its feet, but it was obviously seeking a way of escape. Above it was an arch of clear, pale sky. The sun dried up the trails of blood almost immediately.

"It's like a frantic cockroach in a basin," Andronico muttered to himself.

"What did you say?" his wife asked.

"Nothing, nothing," he replied.

"I wonder why it doesn't go into its cave," remarked Professor Inghirami, calmly noting all the scientific aspects of the scene.

"It's probably afraid of being trapped," suggested Fusti.

"But it must be completely stunned. And I very much doubt whether a Ceratosaurus is capable of such reasoning. A Ceratosaurus—"

"It's not a Ceratosaurus," objected Fusti. "I've restored several for museums, and they don't look like that. Where are the spines on its tail?"

"It keeps them hidden," replied Inghirami. "Look at that swollen abdomen. It tucks its tail underneath and that's why the spines can't be seen.

* * *

---

5. **diminutive** small

As they were talking, one of the hunters, the one who had fired the shot with the cannon, came running toward the terrace where Andronico was, with the evident intention of leaving.

"Where are you going?" shouted Gerol. "Stay in your position until we've finished."

"I'm going," the hunter said firmly. "I don't like it. This isn't what I call hunting."

"What do you mean? That you're afraid?"

"No, sir. I'm not afraid."

"You're afraid, or you'd stay in your place."

"No, I'm not. But you, sir, should be ashamed of yourself."

"Ashamed of myself? You young swine! You're from Palissano, I suppose, and a coward. Get away before I teach you a lesson."

"And where are *you* off to, Beppi?" he shouted, seeing another hunter moving off.

"I'm going too, sir. I don't want to be involved in this horrible business."

"Cowards!" shrieked Gerol. "You'd pay for this if I could get at you!"

"It isn't fear, sir," the second hunter repeated. "This will end badly, you'll see."

"I'll show you how it'll end right now!" Seizing a rock from the ground, the count hurled it at the hunter with all his might. But it missed.

There was a pause while the dragon scrambled about on the rock without managing to climb any higher. Earth and stones gave way and forced it back to its starting point. Apart from the sound of falling stones, there was silence.

Then Andronico spoke. "How much longer is this going to go on?" he shouted to Gerol. "It's fearfully hot. Finish off the animal once and for all, can't you? Why torture it like that, even if it is a dragon?"

"It's not my fault," said Gerol, annoyed. "Can't you see that it's refusing to die? It's got a bullet in its skull, yet it's more lively than ever."

He stopped speaking as the young man they had seen earlier came over the brow of the rock with another goat over his shoulders. Amazed at the sight of the men, their weapons, the traces of blood, and above all the dragon—which he had never seen out of its cave—struggling on the rocks, he stood still in his tracks and stared at the whole strange scene.

"Young man!" Gerol shouted. "How much do you want for the goat?"

"Nothing!" he replied. "I can't sell it! I wouldn't give it to you for its weight in gold. But what have you done to the dragon?" he added, narrowing his eyes to look at the bloodstained monster.

"We're here to settle the matter once and for all. You should be pleased. No more goats in the future."

"Why not?"

"Because the dragon will be dead," said the count, smiling.

"But you can't do that!" exclaimed the young man in terror.

"Don't you start, too," Gerol shouted. "Give me that goat at once."

"I said no," the young man said firmly, drawing back.

The count rushed at him, punched him full in the face, seized the goat from his shoulders, and knocked the young man to the ground.

"You'll regret this one day," the young man said quietly as he picked himself up.

But Count Gerol had already turned his back on him.

Now the whole valley basin was ablaze with the sun's heat, and the glare from the rocks and the stones was such that they could hardly keep their eyes open. There was nothing, absolutely nothing, remotely restful to the eye.

Maria became more and more thirsty, and drink gave no relief. "What heat," she moaned. Even the sight of Count Gerol had begun to pall.[6]

In the meantime dozens of men had appeared, as if they had sprung from the earth itself. They had presumably come up from Palissano at the news that strangers were up at the amphitheater, and they stood motionless on the brows of the various peaks of yellow earth, watching silently.

"Fine audience you've got now," Andronico said in an attempt at a joke, directed at Gerol, who was bending over the goat along with two hunters.

The count looked up and saw the strangers staring at him. He assumed an expression of disdain and continued with what he was doing with the goat.

The dragon, exhausted, had slithered down the rock face onto the gravel. It was lying there, motionless, except for its stomach, which was still throbbing.

"Ready!" shouted one of the hunters, lifting the goat from the ground with Gerol's help. They had opened its stomach and put in an explosive charge with a fuse attached.

The count then moved fearlessly toward the rocks until he was about thirty feet from the dragon, carefully put the goat on the ground, and walked away, unwinding the fuse.

They had to wait for half an hour before the creature moved. The strangers standing on the crests of the hills stood like statues, silent even among themselves, their faces cold with disapproval. Indifferent to the sun, which was now immensely strong, they stared fixedly at the reptile, as though willing it not to move.

But at last the dragon turned suddenly, saw the goat, and dragged itself slowly toward it. It was about to stretch its head and seize the prey when the

---

6. **pall** to lose attraction or interest

count lit the fuse. The spark ran rapidly along it, reached the goat, and the charge exploded.

The report was not loud, much less so than the cannon shots. Yet the dragon's body was hurled violently backward, its belly ripped open. Once again the head began to move slowly from side to side as though it were saying no, it wasn't fair, they had been too cruel, and there was now no more it could do.

The count laughed gleefully, but this time he laughed alone.

"Oh, how awful! That's enough!" Maria gasped, covering her face with her hands.

"Yes," her husband said slowly. "This may end badly."

The monster was lying in a pool of black blood, apparently exhausted. And now from each of its two flanks there rose a column of dark smoke, one on the left and one on the right, two slow-moving plumes rising, it seemed, with difficulty.

"Do you see that?" Inghirami said to his colleague.

"I do," said the other.

"Two blow-holes just like those of the Ceratosaurus, the so-called *operacula hammeriana*."

"No," Fusti said, "it's not a Ceratosaurus."

At this juncture, Gerol emerged from behind the boulder where he had been hiding and came forward to deliver the final blow. He was right in the middle of the stretch of gravel with the iron club in his hand, when the assembled company gave a shriek.

For a moment Gerol thought it was a shout of triumph for the slaying of the dragon. Then he became aware of movement behind him. He turned around sharply and saw two pathetic little creatures tumbling out of the cave and coming toward him at some speed. They were two small reptiles no more than two feet long, diminutive versions of the dying dragon. Two small dragons, its children, probably driven out of the cave by hunger.

It did not take long. The count gave a wonderfully skillful performance.

"Take that! And that!" he shouted gleefully, swinging the iron club. And two blows were enough. Aimed strongly and decisively, the club struck the two little monsters one after the other and smashed their heads like glass bowls. They collapsed and, from a distance, looked like half-deflated bagpipes.

Now the strangers, without a word, turned and fled up the stony gullies, as though from some unexpected danger. Without making a sound, without dislodging a pebble or turning for a moment to look at the dragon's cave, they disappeared as mysteriously as they had come.

Now the dragon was moving again. Dragging itself like a snail and still giving out puffs of smoke, it went toward the two little dead creatures. When it reached them, it collapsed onto the stones, stretched its head with great difficulty, and began to lick them gently, perhaps hoping to resuscitate them.

Finally the dragon seemed to collect all its remaining strength. It raised its neck toward the sky to emit, first very softly, then with rising crescendo, an unspeakable, incredible howl, a sound neither animal nor human, but one so full of loathing that even Count Gerol stood still, paralyzed with horror.

Now they saw why it had not wanted to go back into the cave, where it could have found shelter, and why it hadn't roared or howled, but merely hissed. The dragon was thinking of its children. To save them it had given up its own hope of escape; for if it had hidden in its cave, the men would have followed it and discovered its young; and had it made any noise, the little creatures would have come out to see what was happening. Only now, once it knew they were dead, did the monster give this terrible shriek.

It was asking for the vengeance of its children. But from whom? From the mountains, parched and uninhabited? From the birdless, cloudless sky? From those men who were torturing it? The shriek pierced the walls of the rock and the dome of the sky; it filled the whole world. Unreasonably enough, it seemed impossible that there should be no reply.

"Whom can it be calling?" Andronico asked, trying in vain to adopt a light-hearted tone. "There's no one coming, as far as I can see."

"Oh, if only it would die!" Maria said.

But the dragon would not make up its mind to die, even though Count Gerol, suddenly maddened by the desire to conclude the business once and for all, shot at it with his rifle. Two shots. In vain. The dragon continued to lick its dead children, and slowly, yet surely, a whitish liquid was welling up in its unhurt eye.

"The saurian![7] Professor Inghirami exclaimed. "Look, it's crying!"

Andronico said, "It's late. That's enough, Martino. It's time to go."

Seven times the monster raised its voice, and the rocks and sky resounded. The seventh time it seemed as though the sound were never going to end, but then it suddenly ceased, dropped like a plumbline, and vanished into silence.

* * *

In the deathly quiet that followed there was a sound of coughing. Covered with dust, his face drawn with effort and weariness, Count Gerol, throwing his rifle down among the stones, came across the debris, coughing, with one hand pressed to his chest.

"What is it?" Andronico asked, no longer joking but with a strange presentiment of disaster. "What's happening?"

---

7. **saurian** lizard

"Nothing," Gerol said, trying to sound unconcerned. "I just swallowed a bit of that smoke."

"What smoke?"

Gerol indicated the dragon with his hand. The monster was lying still, its head stretched out on the stones; except for the two slight plumes of smoke, it looked very dead indeed.

"I think it's all over," Andronico said.

It did indeed seem so. The last breath of obstinate life was coming from the dragon's mouth.

No one had answered its call, no one in the whole world had responded. The mountains were quite still, even the diminutive landslides seemed to have stopped, the sky was clear without the slightest cloud, and the sun was setting. No one, either from this world or the next, had come to avenge the massacre. Human beings had blotted out this last remaining stain from the world, human beings so powerful and cunning that wherever they go they establish wise laws for maintaining order, irreproachable human beings who work so hard for the cause of progress and cannot bring themselves to allow the survival of dragons, even in the heart of the mountains; human beings had been the executioners, and recrimination would have been pointless.

What human beings had done was right, absolutely in accordance with the law. Yet it seemed impossible that no one should have answered the last appeal. Andronico, Maria, and the hunters all wanted to escape from the place without more ado; even the two naturalists were willing to give up the usual embalming procedure in order to get away quickly.

The people from the village had disappeared as though they had felt a foreboding of disaster. The shadows climbed the walls of loose rock. The two plumes of smoke continued to rise from the dragon's shriveled carcass, curling slightly in the still air. All seemed over now, an unhappy incident to be forgotten as soon as possible. But Count Gerol went on coughing. Exhausted, he was seated on a boulder, and his friends did not dare to speak to him. Even the fearless Maria averted her gaze. The only sound was his sharp coughing. All attempts at controlling it were unsuccessful; there was a sort of fire burning ever deeper within him.

"I knew it," Andronico whispered to his wife, who was trembling. "I knew it would end badly."

Jane Cahill

Medusa's Story

Angered by Medusa's love for the Greek god Poseidon, the goddess Athena takes revenge by making Medusa's face vile and hideous and by decreeing that anyone who looks at Medusa will turn to stone.

I

TO KNOW YOUR FATE. To glimpse behind the veil of death whilst still alive. To be told how you will die. To understand that you will be hated and feared long after your death. Imagine this. They say that mortal men, long before women were thought of, were given this gift by Prometheus, their creator. Possessing foreknowledge himself, he saw no reason why his men should not know their fates. But imagine. Imagine knowing as you arm yourself before a battle that it will be your last. Imagine knowing that you will kill your own father. However hard you try to avoid it, somewhere, somehow, it will happen. Prometheus' men were not strong enough. Their lives were clouded always by their knowledge, and so Prometheus took his gift away and gave them hope instead.

To know your fate. A curse. My curse. I know that I will die soon, though my sisters try to keep me safe; I know that the mere mention of my name will strike horror into the hearts of mortals for all time. That I will cause harm where I mean no harm, when I bear no grudge, when I have no vengeance in my heart.

We live, my sisters and I, at the very edge of the Earth. We came here long ago, after Athena laid her curse on me. No mortal, man or woman, will ever look on your face and live. That was her curse. And she told me how I would die, and what would happen after.

Why? Why did she hate me? Because Poseidon loved me; because I was beautiful; because she herself can never know the love of a male, man or god.

Poseidon convinced me that he loved me, that we two creatures of the sea should know one another, that I was more beautiful than the daughters of Nereus, that to look on me was for time to stand still. He took me to where there were soft grasses in the woods, fields of white narcissus, like snow in the lowlands, to a grove of oak trees. We made love there and I loved him. He didn't tell me whose trees they were, whose flowers, whose air. Athena's sanctuary desecrated, Athena's home on Earth defiled. Oh gods, I meant no harm. I loved him, that was all. I would have lain with him anywhere on Earth. Must she still punish me? No mortal, man or woman, will ever look on your face and live. I hear her words still in my mind. See her hard grey eyes. Feel her anger.

My sisters found me lying on the grass, alone now, Poseidon gone. My sisters are not mortal. They are unaffected by my face. They can look on me whenever they wish, and when they do they weep. They do not tell me how I look.

One day, not far away now, I will see myself, see my own face reflected, know how hideous I am. And at that moment I will die. So promised Athena.

My sisters took me away to a place where they hope this cannot happen, on the western edge of the Earth. There is little daylight here. It is like living forever in the darkness of the underground. We sleep by day, so that there is no chance I can see my reflection in a lake or a river. No chance for me to play Narcissus. This land is barren like the sea that borders it. No one lives here, save we three.

This is no life, but it is mine: to sleep; to see no living soul; to fear; to know how death will come. I long to look behind its veil, to see the other side. Death could not be a greater torment than this. I want, if truth be told, to know how I look, what monster I am.

Once, I heard footsteps outside our cave and ran to its entrance while my sisters slept. There was a man there. Who he was I do not know—some adventurer, perhaps. Certainly not the one who will bring me my death. And I knew that the curse was indeed on me. He was still in an instant. His body changed to grey granite, his features an image of horror.

If only I could have talked with him awhile, told him who I once was, and how beautiful. Sent him on his way to tell my story to the world. But he is cold stone . . . And I . . . ? There are worse fates than his.

I am in need of sun, of light, of fields of white narcissus. Of some spark of fire to warm me. I am past loving my sisters. We are too much together. Though I will die alone.

And they have seen my face. They know what I do not. How else is solitude to be defined?

II

Athena gave me knowledge of how I will die. Like Prometheus' men, I can scarcely bear it. This is what will happen. A young man—Perseus is his name—will come for me. He is a pleasant young man, who loves his mother and hopes to save her from a distasteful marriage by foiling her suitor. He has no thought of me save that he will kill me without looking at my face. With Athena's help, he will approach the Grey Ones, also my sisters, they whose white hair, white like snow, frames their hideous aged faces, they whose four eyes are sightless save for one which the gods let them share. He will steal from them their eye as they pass it from one to the other, and to get it back from him they will betray me. They will tell him how to find what he needs: a cap of invisibility, so that he can escape when he has killed me; winged shoes so that his flight may be faster; and, most important, a bag to put my head in, to conceal my face so that he will never see it. Athena will give him a curved sword and a shield, her own shield, polished so that it gleams like a mirror.

He will come when we are sleeping. Since that man came, the one who is stone now, my sisters sleep like mothers alert to the cries of their babies, waking at the slightest sound. But they will sleep through this one's approach. Athena will see to that. He will call me, by name, and I will answer him, tell him I am coming. And when I come to the entrance of the cave into the dim light that is all we have of day here, he will turn his eyes away and hold the polished shield up between his face and mine. In the half-light I will see myself and I will know, at last, what I am. For a moment before I die I will know. When I am dead he will cut off my head with his curved blade and place it in his bag without ever looking at my face. My sisters will wake as he leaves. They will find my body, headless, faceless, their hideous child dead in the night, and they will reproach themselves for sleeping too soundly. They will follow Perseus, but will not catch him. Invisible and fleet of foot, he will be gone. My head is not heavy; it will not hold him back.

III

I will be a murderer after my death. How strange a notion; a curse all on its own. My head will be the finest weapon ever known. Perseus will kill the rightful husband of Andromeda, princess of Joppa, when that man comes to his own wedding banquet to claim his bride. Perseus will himself become Andromeda's husband. Then he will return to his own island and kill the king there, who is his mother's despised suitor. Killing them will be easy. He will just show them my face, and they will die.

IV

And I will be known for all time as a monster—people will say that my great eyes bulge, that my hair is a mass of writhing snakes, that I have a boar's tusks on my cheeks, and that my tongue lolls grotesquely from my mouth.

Oh gods, what fate is this? I meant no harm.

Edited by
Minnie Postma

The Woman with the Big Thumbnail

*In this folktale from the Basotho people of southern Africa,
the man-eating monster Machakatane terrorizes the land
until a brave warrior chief tricks her to her death.*

THEY TELL OF MACHAKATANE. Her name tells you that she is a
woman who does not stay at home. No, she wanders around. She is very
rich, this woman. She has cattle. She has sheep. She has goats. But she does
not slaughter any of her animals. The only flesh that she eats is flesh that is
tender—the flesh of humans.

Everybody knew Machakatane. They feared her and hid when they
heard that she was out hunting near them.

When you looked at her she was not ugly. No, she looked just like other
women. There was only one thing that distinguished this maneater-woman
from other women: it was a dreadful thing! It was the nail on the thumb of
her right hand. It was very large. *Yo,* it was so big she could cover a human
being with it, she could squeeze a person to the ground when she wanted to
catch one.

Such a nail had never before been seen on the finger of any other person. And it was hard, that nail, so hard that it could protect its owner when
a spear was thrown at her. *Chè,* when danger came close to Machakatane it
was that nail that she used as a shield.

She went hunting often, this woman. She went far into the mountains
and the regions beyond to hunt. And she killed so many people that she
could not eat them all. She carried the corpses to her home and put them
away in a hut that stood apart from the one in which she lived. It was the
hut of her daughter, Sechakatane. She was a girl who was not yet married.

She had to sleep among those corpses. Every night. Every night. She
shook with fear as she unrolled her sleeping mat among the dead ones, and

with a heart full of terror she lay down and pulled her *karos*, her skin blanket, over her head. When she thought of the corpses she could not sleep.

And it was with that same frightened heart of the night before that she rose every morning. No, she had a hard life. She, Sechakatane. There were also no other people with whom she could talk. When Machakatane was out hunting she was alone in that big village, with all the empty houses, empty because her mother had eaten everybody who had lived there: the adults and the children and the babies. Everybody.

When the chief of that region heard of the murders that this woman had committed his anger was great. But he was a brave chief and decided to attack the maneater. *Yoalo.* Just so.

He called his warriors together. He called them together, and then he chose the bravest among them. They took their weapons and their dogs, and with their chief they drew up toward Machakatane.

They stalked her village. But they went no nearer than the deep canyon that cut through the mountains near her village. There the big man let his men hide among the bushes. They and their dogs. It was only he who walked alone to the village of the maneater. He walked very cautiously. He stayed above the wind, so say the old people, because you have to be very careful of anyone with such a big nail on the thumb.

When the chief approached the village, he listened. He listened, but he heard no sounds of people. A great silence lay among the huts. He peeped through the chinks in the reed screens in front of the huts to see what the people were doing, but he saw no one. It was empty behind the screens. And there were no fires burning. Everything was quiet. *Tu-u-u-u.*

Chief Bulane now knew that it had been the truth that he had heard about Machakatane: she had eaten all her own people, and that was why the village was empty, and silence reigned even inside the screens.

Hm! He did not know what to do. Where would he find that woman? He walked among the huts, and then he heard a woman's voice singing:

> *Hiii-hiii-hiii-ai!*
> *Hiii-hiii-hiii-ai!*

He went closer to the voice. It came from behind the screen in front of the biggest hut in the village. He went nearer. He went nearer. He went nearer.

He peeped through the reeds of the shelter. There he saw a girl sitting. She was beautiful, but she was very thin. She was black from thinness. It was she who sang so sadly:

Hiii-hiii-hiii-ai!
Hiii-hiii-hiii-ai!

He went in by the opening in the screen, and when she saw him she was frightened and wanted to flee like an animal that is startled from its sleep, but he talked nicely to her. He put her at ease, and when her heart had lain down Bulane again spoke to her. He asked politely:

"Who are you, Mother?"

And she replied: "I am the daughter of Machakatane, *Morena*, my master. But you must flee, Father. That woman will kill you for your flesh if she finds you here. It is nearly time for her to return."

But he said he would hide. He would wait for her. *Yoalo. Yoalo.*

"Where will you hide, *Morena*? Her nose will tell her that a human is here."

"I will sit in your sleeping hut, and then she will think it is you that she smells."

"*Au, Morena,* you cannot go in there. My hut is the place where the dead are kept, the meat for Machakatane!"

"*Chè,*" said he, "then we must not look for another place for me to hide. The smell of my body will make friends with the smell of the dead ones. She will never know that a live person is sitting with her meat."

So say the old people. And, when the girl saw how brave he was and how wisely he spoke, her respect for him grew. When she heard the footfalls of Machakatane, she hid Bulane in the darkness of her hut, behind all the dead ones who were there.

Machakatane came there. She did not know of Bulane who sat so still with all the dead ones. She ate quickly and went out to hunt again.

When she had gone, the girl Sechakatane called to Bulane so that he could come out.

He did so, and then he went to the corrals where the cattle were, there where Machakatane's great herds were. He let them come out. All of them. And they were many, so say the old people. Bulane put Sechakatane on the back of an ox, and they drove the cattle to the canyon where his men were waiting for him.

But the way was long. And it was dry. The hoofs of the great herd of cattle loosened the hard-packed earth and sent great clouds of dust into the air. The maneater saw the red clouds against the sky. And she knew it was her cattle being driven away.

She did not wait. She followed them. So say the old people. She ran after them, and, when Sechakatane saw how the huge nail on her thumb reflected the rays of the sun like a pool of water, she became afraid, but Bulane calmed her.

"You must let your heart lie down, Mè," said he. "I shall see that no harm comes to you."

When Machakatane came close to them, he caused a great row of trees to appear between them, a row of trees that stretched all the way up the canyon. So say the old people.

Bulane and Sechakatane climbed into the tree nearest to them. When the old woman came to the tree she saw them sitting in the branches. She laughed, because she thought she had them in her power. She laughed, she laughed, and then she started to cut down the tree with that hard nail on her thumb. But just as the tree was about to fall, the two fugitives jumped into the tree that was the second tree in the row.

Machakatane saw them. She saw them and she began to cut down the trunk of that second tree also with her nail, just like the first one. *Yoalo.* Just so. But before she could catch Bulane and her daughter, they jumped into the branches of the next tree.

And so it kept on. So it kept on. Until the two fugitives sat in the last tree in the canyon. The maneater cut that trunk also with her nail. She did not know of the danger that waited for her. *Twah!* she cut. *Twah, twah!*

Then Bulane called to his men, who had been sitting as quietly as partridges between the bushes.

"Bring your dogs," he commanded. "Set them on that woman!"

They did so. *Yoalo. Yoalo.*

When the dogs attacked her she used that thumbnail of hers as a shield. She hid behind it, so say the old people. But it could not protect her. When the dogs were in front, the warriors would attack from behind. And, when she held the shield between herself and the warriors, the dogs would attack from behind. Just so. *Yoalo. Yoalo.*

They killed Machakatane. They killed her well, so that she could not come alive again. The dogs tore her apart and ate her flesh as she had eaten the flesh of so many people.

When the danger was over, Bulane took the young girl to his village. His wives fed her with much food and she grew fat. She was so fat she was yellow in the face. She shone, so beautiful was she. And Bulane divided the cattle of the maneater between her and himself. She was now not only a beautiful girl, but she also had much cattle.

Bulane's big *induna*, Bulane's big warrior chief, saw Sechakatane and loved her. He drove much cattle from his own herd to that of Bulane, to pay for Sechakatane. And the chief gave her to the *induna* as wife, so they say, because she did not have a father or a big brother who could give her away.

They held a great feast to celebrate the marriage of Sechakatane and the *induna*; many oxen and sheep were slaughtered, many clay pots of beer were brewed. And the young people danced and sang for many days and nights on end. Such a big feast had never been held in that land.

After the feast was over, the *induna* and his bride and many other people went back to the village of Machakatane, enough people to fill all the empty huts again. And they took their cattle with them, so say the old people. Enough cattle to fill all the empty corrals again.

The *induna* then became chief over all the people and of the whole territory that had belonged to the maneater-woman. And Sechakatane was his first and most important wife.

And here the story finds an end.

Ke tsomo ka mathetho, which means: this is a true tale of the Basotho people.